Some of us like to live by the ...
impressions. In this book, Ri[c] ...
deep, scholarly reading of the ~~book and the experience~~
in the Spirit. With his zany sense of humour and his experience of life as a hippie and then, since his conversion, as a student, long-serving pastor and Bible teacher, he brings together Word and Spirit. I recommend meditating on one chapter a day in your walk with the Lord.

Dr Thomas A. Noble, research professor of theology at Nazarene Theological Seminary, Kansas City and senior research fellow in theology at Nazarene Theological College, Manchester

Can anything good come out of Woodstock? This witty zinger, taken from the book, exemplifies Richard's self-knowing sense of humour, which lightly skips across every page, threading a path through passages of deep wisdom and insight. To meet Richard is to be ever grateful for having done so. If you haven't met him in person, meet him in the pages of this book – and let him set up a meeting for you with the person this book is really about. Can anything good come out of Woodstock? I have to say, it most certainly has.

Andy Kind, author, preacher and comedian

Until I read this book, I had never thought, 'The secret to a meaningful life is to be awesome every day.' However, now I realize what this means and how long it takes to be such a person! Richard writes in a fresh manner, and I found the book gripping from start to finish. It is engaging and humorous, but it has an important message to share with us all. In this AI world, I love his mention of the 'divine microchip' in each of us. *'Their eternity-microchip tracker is beeping more than ever as the world continues to spiral into chaos and mayhem. They may not express it in front of us, but inside they are all looking up and shouting, "There must be more than this!"'* I was challenged to lean deeper into God rather than relying on my own abilities and knowledge. He lives in us by his Spirit and is most glorified when we live in harmony with him. Truly, the world needs an encounter with God's awesome people, clothed with Christ and full of the Holy Spirit. Then, when they ask us why we're different, may we be bold enough to tell them about Jesus, our Saviour, their only hope and source of lasting contentment.

David Whitmarsh, partnerships manager (NI)
at Compassion UK

I first met the author, Richard Porter, in 1984 while serving in Israel with Project Kibbutz. Even back then, it was clear that Richard was a humble and wise man, transformed by Jesus Christ. This book is not about a theological system but about a practical, biblical way of living in the Holy Spirit. It's written for every believer who wants to see the awesomeness of God in their life. It's fresh water for the thirsty.

Paulo de Angelo, retired pastor with the Presbyterian
Independent Church of Brazil and Evangelical Community of
Limeira-São Paulo; co-founder of Kayros Mission

I don't want safety. I want risk and adventure. I want to live in such a way that when people see what happens, they say, 'Did you just see what God did?' Richard's book is a catalyst that inspires me to continue on that God-led adventure, a journey that lets others see God and points them to Jesus. I encourage you to read it and let the Holy Spirit set your heart on fire for the adventure of a lifetime!

Revd Alan Kilpatrick, team member of Family Care
at Iris Global

I've known Richard for over fifteen years, so this endorsement is for more than a book; it is for a man who is always looking to hook an 'extra' onto the 'ordinary' things in our lives and churches. I remember hearing in 2016 that he had 'officially retired'. I laughed to myself and thought, 'Retire? No chance; he's got years of adventure left in him!' This book is a powerful expression of his journey as a pastor, pilgrim, evangelist and friend. It is exactly what I needed to read, and this book, I feel, is something we all need to read. Prolific with words and captivating stories, biblically solid, and a radical invitation for each of us to allow the Holy Spirit to breathe into our deflated forms of Christianity. This book will awaken faith, inspire adventure, and help everyone who reads it step into a daily perpetual expectation of being truly awesome.

Mitch, evangelist and co-founder of Crown Jesus Ministries

THE ADVENTURE-DRIVEN *Life*

Reclaiming the awesomeness of God every day

RICHARD PORTER

Authentic

First published 2024 by Authentic Media Limited,
PO Box 6326, Bletchley, Milton Keynes, MK1 9GG.
authenticmedia.co.uk

British Library Cataloguing in Publication Data
A catalogue record for this book is available from the British Library.
ISBN: 978-1-78893-358-2
978-1-78893-359-9 (e-book)

All stories in this book are true; some names and identifying details have been
changed to protect the privacy of the individuals involved.

Cover design by Luigi
Printed and bound by CPI Group (UK) Ltd, Croydon, CR0 4YY

Copyright Acknowledgements

- Word: What *did* Jesus do?
- Word and Principle: What *would* Jesus do?
- Word and Spirit: What *is* Jesus asking me to do?

For those who are led by the Spirit of God are the children of God.

(Rom. 8:14)

Wanderlust of heaven, awaken my soul.
With the boldness of prayer help me let go.
Lord, can I climb out of the boat?
Come, my child, I'll keep you afloat –
Let the adventure begin.

Richard Porter

Contents

Introduction   1

Part One   The Call   **5**
  1. Chicken in the Car   7
  2. Shocker   11
  3. Intolerable Seizure   14
  4. Oil Shortage   16
  5. Wonder upon Wonder   22
  6. Ticket to Ride   27
  7. Green Light   30
  8. Clocks and Watches   33
  9. Uber Encounter   35

Part Two   The Wardrobe   **37**
  10. Masks in the Closet   39
  11. Put It On   42
  12. Follow the Smoke   46
  13. Take It Off   49
  14. Anointed Threads   53
  15. Twilight Zone   57
  16. Art of Growing Up   62

Part Three   The Matrix   67

  17. Cajoled to Despair   69
  18. What's It All About?   73
  19. Divine Microchip   78
  20. Face in the Mirror   83
  21. Slow the Descent   90
  22. Reality Gauge   95
  23. Be Christ in the Room   98

Part Four   The Identity   103

  24. Sword of Freedom   105
  25. Who are You?   108
  26. I Pledge Allegiance   111
  27. Kingdom Accountability   114
  28. True to His Word   118
  29. Heaven's Lesson   124
  30. Heaven's Income   128
  31. Heaven's Priority   131

Part Five   The Snapshots   135

  32. Look   137
  33. Listen   144
  34. Gamble   150
  35. Pray   153
  36. Love   158
  37. Worship   161
  38. Obey   166
  39. Think   173
  40. Laugh   176
  41. Give   182

42.	Serve	187
43.	Restore	192
44.	Walk	199
45.	Stand	204
46.	Declare	211
	Epilogue	214
	Notes	218

This book unapologetically wants to resuscitate the word 'awesome'. A generation captured it, exploited it, chewed it up, spat it out, and now it lies dormant as linguistic road kill. It's the victim of a verbal fling: overused, underwhelmed, and misappropriated. The cadaver is sometimes exhumed for sarcastic hyperbole, but the demise of this majestic word is a crime, a violation of vocal and written protocol.

Ha! Now that I've got that off my chest, I just want to confirm that this really is a book honouring God: Father, Son, and Holy Spirit. My previous publication, *The Kingdom of God: The Director's Cut*, was about the community; this volume is about the citizens of the kingdom, the individuals who live in that community.

Have you ever asked Jesus if you could call down fire on your enemies or the unbelievers of this world? James and John, the disciples of Jesus did. Of course, Jesus quickly quashed that idea – it's just not Christian.

Have you ever asked Jesus to reserve the highest place of honour in heaven for you, sitting next to him in glory? Some of his disciples did, along with their mother's pleading. Jesus didn't tell them to stop thinking or dreaming like this; no, he just explained that he wasn't the one to grant that position. Have you ever asked Jesus to buoy you up so you could walk on water? Peter did. Jesus didn't stop him. He just said, 'Come.'

What happened to these followers of Jesus? They never talked like this before they met him. They said their prayers, but nothing was as outrageous as these requests. The disciples obviously had a spiritual upgrade. Their expectation level had received an adrenaline boost from heaven. It seems the sky was no longer the limit – they'd obviously outgrown this world.

Walking with Jesus, they witnessed miraculous events they never dreamed possible. The vista of who they were and what they could be with Jesus astounded them. The possibilities were endless. The longer they lived in the presence of the Lord, the Lord of Glory, the more they envisioned what that glory could look like in their lives and on this planet. They could actually be like Jesus, striding into the miraculous, doing what he does, saying what he says, and believing what he believes – and they were actually doing it. The adventure was theirs.

Can we possibly be like Jesus this side of eternity? The Bible not only says we should, but it also tells us this is God's expectation and goal for us – it's our destiny. Isn't this what Jesus taught his disciples? This book explores that destiny. It's an adventure of grace, love, hope and danger.

My hope and prayer are that this book will trigger in us what Jesus triggered in his disciples. They no longer defined themselves by the choice of their career. They rose above that. The synagogue was no longer the umpire directing their lives and spiritual expectations. They broke through those boundaries and yet remained true to God and his Messiah. They were excited, stimulated and awakened to the possibilities Jesus held out to them. They were hungry for more. They were thirsty and unmoored from the shores of complacency and mediocrity. They found what they had been looking for and desiring all their lives. They were living in the tangible presence of God and doing the God things they never thought possible this side of eternity.

Their anticipation level exponentially shot through the roof of conventional, cultivated regularities. May God inspire our aspirations the way he did these first disciples. May this level of faith and desire rise up in each one of us who calls on the name of Jesus. Life is short. I pray we never have to look back in remorse, wishing we had taken more faith risks for God and his kingdom.

So, in all my humbled humbleness, I present to the reader snapshots of what this adventurous Christian life can be and what it could look like. The theology that supports such a life is also addressed and explored. It's wonderful. It overcomes the world. It's miraculous. It's fun. It's full of joy, and it reveals the heart of God to a spiritually confused world. It's attractive to those who are searching for the reality of God in their lives. The adventure-driven life is truly awesome. Let's not just resurrect the word 'awesome' but let's resurrect the lifestyle that word so aptly describes. Yee-haw!

PART ONE
The Call

1. Chicken in the Car

Embarrassing moments are embarrassing, duh! I have had so many it would be humiliating to list them, but I will tell you this one story because it keeps me humble and grounded in a funky sort of way.

Two years ago, a week before Christmas, my wife and I drove to the supermarket to buy a chicken for the evening meal. As usual for winter, it was rainy, dark and cold outside. My wife was driving, and the car park was busy. We eventually found a spot, and my wife insisted she wasn't getting out of the car. To maintain a healthy relationship, I went, drafted to face the elements alone and hunt down the bird that would feed us. You know the drill: manly men doing manly things. So I bought the fowl and carried it out of the store. It wasn't in a shopping bag. I had made the kill and carried my trophy with pride for all to see and admire: a model husband bringing back food from the hunt for his hungry family.

Sadly, my triumphant return was short-lived. The rain was pelting my face and clouding my glasses, and I didn't have a clue where we had parked the car. Hurriedly, I walked up and down, row after row, looking for our blue Ford.

Soaked, cold and befuddled, I eventually found it. Relieved, I knocked on the passenger window, waiting for the familiar click of the lock release. It came, and I threw open the door, tossed the chicken on the floor, bounced into the seat, fastened my seatbelt, and spoke: 'OK, I'm ready; let's go!'

No answer. No ignition. No response. I looked over to the driver's seat, and there was a bearded man staring at me. I was in the wrong car.

After the initial shock, we both burst out laughing. Then I picked up the bird, jumped out of the seat, and said, 'Well, thanks for the virtual ride. At least you'll have a story to tell your family when you get home.' I could still hear him laughing as I continued my search for the real blue Ford. Be awesome – heh!

When eventually I was seated next to my wife, she asked, 'What took you so long?' Reluctantly, I told her my tale of angst and woe. She just smiled, shook her head, and exclaimed, 'What planet are you on?'

That's when I reached into my mighty biblical arsenal and blurted out, 'I am not of this world, and I have a higher authority that confirms it.' Eyes were rolled and the car moved off.

For some mortifying reason, the following Sunday I tailored that chicken story into my sermon. Out of curiosity, I asked the congregation if anything like this had ever happened to them. Amid the audible sniggers, no one raised a hand, and I watched some of the heads move side to side to emphasize, 'Nope, I never did anything that stupid.'

What can I say? On reflection, I admit the chicken incident was just a random, silly mistake, but the question it triggered is worth exploring. What planet am I on?

Jesus said he wasn't of this world.[1] Next, he tells us we aren't of this world.[2] After which he declares, the kingdom of God is not of this world.[3] It seems that our feet stand on good old terra firma, but we don't really belong here. We have become strangers in a strange land.

We are instructed to loosen our hold on the world we can touch and experience with all our inflamed senses, and then we are to squeeze ourselves into the world our eyes have never seen.[4] Navigating between these two realms has never been easy. We all struggle with it – even with an open Bible.[5]

Jesus left some very big footprints on this planet, but they always led to the kingdom of God. We also leave our mark on the world. Where our footprints lead is being evaluated at this present moment. What planet are we on? How do we live day by day in a crazy, messy, chaotic world and keep our boat steady and afloat in the unseen world we are reborn into?

The answer is simple. Don't settle for a safe, common, featureless, mundane and powerless lifestyle that speaks the name of Jesus but leaves him in heaven waiting at the gate for us to arrive. Some consider this the normal Christian life, but God never sanctioned it, and he never will. This may sound outrageous and over the top, but God has called us to be awesome in this world because our resources in him transcend everything this present world can provide.

We have the joy of Jesus.[6] It's not of this world. We have the peace that passes this world's understanding.[7] We aren't bound by the physics of this planet.[8] We have open communication with the Creator of the universe. He listens. He answers our requests. We have an open channel that the world has a hard time tapping into. We have the Holy Spirit, the life, heart and mind of Christ in our mortal body. We are already awesome *in* this world, but we need to *be* awesome in this world.

I'm not trying to stroke our egos. As a matter of fact, if we live up to it, we will see how humbling and self-effacing it actually is to live a life worthy of the salvation Jesus afforded us.

Let's not domesticate our faith. That's like tossing a dead chicken on the floor of a parked car. We can sit there amused while the devils laugh it up and pull our seatbelts a bit tighter, but this is not the awesome life God has planned for us. Instead, let's get out and seek the real deal. The adventure is before us. This is what brings glory to God. Anything less is just marking time, hoping to get whisked away with as little effort and discomfort as possible. People like to quote Psalm 14:1: 'The fool says in his heart, "There is no God."' However, I would say the greater fool is the person who says there is a God but lives as though God wasn't there. That is a tragedy.

Shocker

During my hippie phase, my favourite paperback was *A Child's Garden of Grass*. It was my hippie bible. Ooo – now I wonder what that book was about?[1]

For the record, I no longer toke on the bong[2] or participate in such activities, but I still have a vestige of 1960s' hippie-ness lurking in me. It's not a demon! It's a childlike wanderlust to be free from the world and the standards, laws and wars that drive it.

I no longer have Samson's hair because all my cherished follicles have abandoned ship. DNA was my Delilah. I have been unrelentingly clipped by nature, but I still resist domestication and conformity. I just can't bow to a world system that tries to dupe, defraud and seduce me into a cage that God never intended any of his image-bearers to crawl into.

When I first crossed over to the kingdom of God as a fully fledged member and follower of Jesus Christ, I was transformed. I was finally able to lift my head above the mist and see the spiritual machinations that drive this world and reassess my position in it from the Creator's perspective.

In 1975, I laid down my well-worn hippie bible and picked up the one inspired by God. Since my change of heart, I now march to the beat of a different drum, and I have learned things that have helped me to walk in this world and not be a part of it. Things that bring hope in hopeless situations. Things taught to me by the Holy Spirit and the real Bible.

At times I feel my heart is being renewed quicker than my head, and it's hard to keep up. I once confessed to my wife, 'Well, my love, whatever comes out of my mouth is news to me.' Obviously, some words are wiser than others.[3] This, too, is something I've learned over time.

A few weeks ago, I told my friends and family that I had found the true meaning of life. They were curious, so I enlightened them. 'The secret to a meaningful life is to be awesome every day.' As you can imagine, their guffaws were quite unsettling. Obviously, I was speaking to a room full of loveable sceptics who smirk and quote it back to me. My cousin wants to print it on a T-shirt. Have I won over the detractors? Is the statement true? Is it even possible to be awesome every day? I think, for many, the notion is ludicrous.

A week later, what started as a joke began to percolate in my brain. Is there anything in the Bible about this 'awesome' thingy? To my surprise, as I flicked through the sacred pages, it was everywhere. Of course, it's couched in Jewish lingo, but it's present throughout.

Be holy because I, the LORD your God, am holy.

(Lev. 19:2)

You are the light of the world . . . let your light shine before others, that they may see your good deeds and glorify your Father in heaven.

(Matt. 5:14–16)[4]

Be perfect, therefore, as your heavenly Father is perfect.

(Matt. 5:48)

And we all, who with unveiled faces contemplate the Lord's glory, are being transformed into his image with ever-increasing glory, which comes from the Lord, who is the Spirit.

(2 Cor. 3:18)

But just as he who called you is holy, so be holy *in all you do*; for it is written: 'Be holy, because I am holy.'

(1 Pet. 1:15–16, italics mine)[5]

Imitate God, therefore, *in everything you do*, because you are his dear children.

(Eph. 5:1, NLT, italics mine)

In this world we are like Jesus.

(1 John 4:17)

But if anyone obeys his word, love for God is truly made complete in them. This is how we know we are in him: whoever claims to live in him must live as Jesus did.

(1 John 2:5–6)[6]

Shocker! Be like God. Be holy in the same way that God is holy. Be perfect in the same way God is perfect. Imitate God in everything you do. Be like Jesus. The fact that we were created in his image adds to the weight and possibility of such a spiritual enterprise. God is awesome. We are called to be awesome every day. I find it interesting that no one laughed when God first said it.

Each generation tends to hijack the English language. We did it in the sixties and seventies. We used words like, 'bummer', 'cool', 'groovy', 'freak', 'turn on', 'downer', and 'heavy'. Young people do it today. When my sons were growing up, they would come home saying, 'That was beast.' I'd just smile and nod like an uneducated troglodyte. I must confess, being cool nowadays is more difficult than it used to be. Since becoming a parent, I stopped trying.

It seems that each generation births its own dictionary of encoded words. What gets me, though, is when a great word is hijacked and we're left with nothing to replace it. It's just not right. It's like a smile without a front tooth or a spoken sentence with an empty pause.

The other day, someone posted a picture of their lunch on Facebook. The caption read, 'This cheeseburger is awesome.' Whaaa –? Awesome? A burger? When God said, 'Let there be light', that was awesome. When our telescopes give us photos of the universe or the Horsehead Nebula,[1] we gaze in awe. When someone gets up out of their wheelchair and starts to run, that too is awesome. It's awesome because it overwhelms us. Our jaws drop. We are astonished. It's breath-taking, staggering, and magnificent – but a cheeseburger? The only reason my jaw drops for a cheeseburger is to take a bite, not to stamp it with some galactic commendation.

The word 'awesome' has been hijacked without a replacement, and we, as Christians, need to grab it back, not just to spice up our vocabulary but for the direction of our lives. What other word can fully express the emotion and wonder one has when they encounter or think about the Creator of heaven and earth, the One who called us to be like him?

God is awesome. Jesus lived an awesome life, and so did his followers. The Holy Spirit does awesome things. The miracles, the life, the sacrifices, and the words from heaven left people speechless.[2] I don't want to just reclaim the word 'awesome'. I hope to rescue the quality of life it describes. It is an otherworldly adventure on the shores of earth. This is our God-given destiny. To languish in religious mediocrity slays the soul. We are called to be supernovas, not black holes, or semi-idolaters worshipping the perfect lunch. When the word of God is spoken in the power of the Holy Spirit, people are awed, rendered speechless, healed, saved and baptized.

Have we missed something regarding our calling as followers of Jesus Christ? Have we settled for a pedestrian church life, thinking this is it?

> If I can only make it to the finish line. I may stumble along the way but I signed the contract, so I'll sing the songs and do good deeds like a respectable Christian should.

We may have surrendered the word 'awesome' to a younger generation, but we can't surrender its impact on the Christian life. We are called to be awesome every day. Our lifestyle and expectations draw their inspiration and potential from the presence of God, not from ourselves. The presence of God is what inspired and motivated the early disciples, before and after the ascension.[3] Be awesome, because I will be awesome through you. Be perfect, because I am perfect in you. Be holy because I am holy; Christ in you is the hope of glory.

Oil Shortage

The more we live outside God's tangible presence, the quicker the lights go out. Disillusionment creeps in and takes over the life we once loved. We go to church and participate, but inside we know we aren't present. The lamp is leaking oil, and the world is becoming more attractive than singing the songs and listening to a TED[1] talk from the pulpit. We feel like the person who crashed the wedding party, but is no longer dressed for the occasion.[2] We've moved on and left God behind – or maybe God has moved on. Either way, there's a disconnect. Heaven feels distant, and it seems like the good Lord has taken the joy and excitement with him – bummer.

If you have ever felt this way, you are not alone. The disorder is widespread, and God is on it. He lets us run on empty for a while to awaken our spiritual hunger. Just read the parable of the prodigal son. It's enlightening on many levels.[3] Consider the story of the wise and foolish virgins.[4]

Ten were standing on the road with lamps in hand, waiting to welcome the bridegroom. They all wanted to go indoors to the wedding bash. You couldn't tell the ten apart until some of the lamps started to flicker. So the five running on empty went to the wise virgins and asked for a top-up: 'Give us some of your oil; our lamps are going out.'[5]

This mindset follows people in and out of church doors all the time. 'I'm just not being fed in the other place, so I thought I would come here for a while.' Or in other words, 'Give me some of your oil; my lamp is going out.'

What's alarming in this parable is the ratio. If we were telling the story we'd probably say eight or nine were wise, and a small minority were foolish, but Jesus said it was half and half. Only one half would enter the doors. This I find disconcerting. Perhaps those doors are narrower than we think.

> Then Jesus went through the towns and villages, teaching as he made his way to Jerusalem. Someone asked him, 'Lord, are only a few people going to be saved?'
>
> He said to them, 'Make every effort to enter through the narrow door, because many, I tell you, will try to enter and will not be able to. Once the owner of the house gets up and closes the door, you will stand outside knocking and pleading, "Sir, open the door for us."
>
> But he will answer, "I don't know you or where you come from."'
>
> *(Luke 13:22–5)*

If this disquiets us, be encouraged. It's a good sign the Holy Spirit is speaking. When the Spirit knocks it's not always comfortable; but it sure is necessary.

So, what do we normally do when the tank is close to empty? We usually rush to the new-start congregation down the road, or we scan the internet for the latest podcasts, or we search out the Christian celebrity who's more than willing to share a bit of their oil. We look for special events or new authors, or we seek out a word of knowledge from those who apparently have a bit more oil than ourselves. This is not a bad thing. It shows us God is with us, and we are hungry and desire fire in the soul. However, this oil will quickly dissipate because we're skirting the issue and missing the main point.

I'm pleased Jesus is telling the story and not us. We'd probably insert a Christian response and cloud the message. 'Then, with deep compassion, the wise virgins started to share their oil with the less fortunate. What started with a few drops to get them through the night gained momentum. It's now a global ministry in support of the luministically challenged.' Yee-haw!

However, this isn't the way it went down. The surprising twist is that the wise virgins don't want to share. 'No. Go to those who sell oil and buy some for yourselves.'[6] Is that an un-Christlike attitude? Is this the message: Don't share with those who ask for help? Don't give? Look out for yourself and your own salvation? No, not at all. The key to the whole parable is to go to the source. Go to those who sell. They always have enough for everyone. Don't rely on us. Our supply is also limited and often needs replenishing.

Do we get it? Jesus is telling us that if the fire is going out, don't run to others; run to him. He's the fountain. Be patient, pray and listen. Give him your time, your worship and your devotion. Allow him to perpetually fill you. Don't rush away to third parties. Go to him without reservation. Don't look to others to relight the flame. Make the time and effort to seek him out face-to-face. He will communicate with us directly if we look to him and listen. Connect with him. He is here for us. He will fill us. He wants us to get to know him – to dig deeper. This is fundamental if we want to reclaim the awesomeness of God in our lives.

Jesus answered, 'Everyone who drinks this water will be thirsty again, but whoever drinks the water *I give them* will never thirst. Indeed, the water *I give them* will become in them a spring of water welling up to eternal life.'

(John 4:13–14, italics mine)

Jesus declared, 'I am the bread of life. Whoever *comes to me* will never go hungry, and whoever believes in me will never be thirsty.'

(John 6:35, italics mine)

'Let anyone who is thirsty *come to me* and drink. Whoever believes in me, as Scripture has said, rivers of living water will flow from within them.' By this he meant the Spirit, whom those who believed in him were later to receive.

(John 7:37–9, italics mine)

I once went to a Christian tent meeting. The speaker was fluent, accurate and precise in his 'word of knowledge'. It was amazing. He said to the person next to me, 'I see you and two other people breaking into a drug store.' Then he listed the drugs they took. 'God is calling you to repent right now and get your heart right with him.' What amazed me even more is that the person next to me fell to his knees and started to pray. The speaker then focused on me and told me things I will never forget.

A few days later, I went back to that tent to receive another word from God. Why not? I wanted everything that God had to give. After the sermon, he asked people to come forward for prayer. I went to the front with all the others. God was there. Then my turn came. I was ready to hear and receive but, to my dismay, the speaker skipped past me as though I wasn't there. He ministered to the person on my left and the one on my right, but he ignored me.

As I left the tent, I was praying, wondering why I had been left out. I felt God say that he didn't want me searching for others to give me a word. He wanted me to listen to him directly. That was such a valuable lesson. Go to the source. I thank God that the speaker was sensitive enough to pass me by.

The way to an awesome life is in the presence of God. Outside the presence of God, knowledge becomes academic. Action outside of his presence tends to digress into a work of the flesh. Spiritual activity without God is empty religion.[7] This is not what feeds our souls, produces oil or light, or brings the anointing of the Holy Spirit. It's Jesus we need to connect with. God gave us teachers and spiritually gifted people to minister, but our eyes are to be focused on God working through them, not the minister. A close encounter of the spiritual kind is what opens the door to an awesome life and rouses the adventure.

> If your Presence does not go with us, do not send us up from here. How will anyone know that you are pleased with me and with your people unless you go with us? *What else will distinguish me and your people from all the other people on the face of the earth?*
> *(Exod. 33:15–16, italics mine)*

Moses was constantly living in the presence of God; substitutes will not suffice.[8] Earlier, God told him he would send an angel to lead them into Canaan, but that wasn't good enough.[9] Moses wanted to encounter God face-to-face, not through a representative. He was saying, 'I don't want the go-between; I want you. I'm not leaving here unless you go with us.' Moses went directly to the source, and that pleased God.[10] His lamp was full and burning bright, and the followers who wanted all their divine encounters second-hand were always running to him for oil.[11]

We could learn a lot from Moses.

When awe and wonder no longer describe our experience and life with God, he is concerned. Listen to what he told his people in Israel when routine replaced the presence of God in their lives and worship.

> These people come near to me with their mouth
>   and honour me with their lips,
>   but their hearts are far from me.
> Their worship of me
>   is based on merely human rules they have been taught.
> Therefore once more I will astound [awe] these people
>   *with wonder upon wonder*;
> the wisdom of the wise will perish,
>   the intelligence of the intelligent will vanish.
>
> *(Isa. 29:13–14, italics mine)*

I love the shrewdness of God. When the Jewish nation lost its passion, God said, 'Once more I will astound these people with wonder upon wonder.' In other words, he's going to re-awaken their vision of what he is like and who he is, and it will be astounding. It's exciting. It's revival. This is what enticed Moses to go to the bush, Peter to walk on water, and Paul to convert.

The moment routine drifts into monotony, we probably need to change the routine. When duty overtakes joy, perhaps, it's time to evaluate our commitment. But when the gears of the Holy Spirit adventure grind to a standstill, then it's time to pray: 'Lord, show me your glory. Overwhelm me yet again with wonder upon wonder.' Then brace yourself. Be ready to jump out of the boat to follow, and don't look back.

This is how God breaks people out of empty religion. He overwhelms them with awesome acts and a greater revelation of who he is and what he can and will do.[1] The judicious and the wise will not be able to explain it or fully understand the mystery of God and his ways. This is what happens in most revivals.

The Layman's Prayer Revival of 1857–8 saw at least a million people come to Christ. It started in New York and spread throughout the United States and beyond. It was a prayer movement. Some of the prayer meetings hosted ten thousand or more participants. It promoted unity, reconciliation, and a strong desire for personal and social transformation. When ships started to dock in New York harbour, sailors were convicted and saved by God before they stepped off the boat. On college campuses, there was revival after revival – wonder upon wonder.

The Azusa Street Revival of 1906 reawakened the church to the gifts of the Holy Spirit and the miraculous. The gift of tongues was aroused. This was the beginning of the Pentecostal movement – wonder upon wonder.

The Hebrides Revival that began in 1949 was a miraculous move of God. People would wake up in the middle of the night, sensing the fear of God upon them. They flocked to church without invitation. There were more people standing outside the building than inside it. The building wasn't large enough to hold the crowds. Hundreds were converted before they entered the doors or heard a sermon – wonder upon wonder.

The Jesus movement is an incredible story of wonder upon wonder as God saves a lost generation. Multitudes of hippies and young people throughout North America and beyond were turning to Jesus. It spanned the late sixties into the seventies, some say into the eighties. Its counter-cultural influence is still with us today. The movement was devoted to evangelism and the imminent return of Jesus Christ. I remember it well.

There are, of course, many other Christian revivals and movements throughout the world that could be mentioned. However, in all great revivals, God is breaking into his church with wondrous acts of love and grace; and it confounds the wisdom of the wise. All these revivals challenged the status quo. They are radical movements, but God is at the helm. Wonder upon wonder will confound the wise and stymie the intelligent, but each one reawakens the church to the glory of God.

God cannot be packaged or contained. He may break out of our theological expectations, but he will stay true to the loving, just and holy Father he is. It's hard to imagine an awesome life if we lose sight of the awesome God who lives that life in and through us. God wants to live with us; revival is when we let him.

If you are curious about God's 'wonder upon wonder' operation in the Old Testament, just read a bit further in Isaiah 29. He prophetically unveils the consequence.

They will keep my name holy;
>   they will acknowledge the holiness of the Holy One of Jacob,
>   and will *stand in awe* of the God of Israel.
They who are wayward in spirit will gain understanding;
>   those who complain will accept instruction.

>   *(Isa. 29:23–4, italics mine)*

God will not let his people drift away from him. We are so easily distracted. When our eyes are not focused on him, God will get our attention one way or another. This is love. This is dedication. This is commitment. This is his blessing upon us. He has impeccable ways to connect with us and keep us. As Jesus said, 'No one will snatch [you] out of my hand.'[2]

Here are the words of an unrecorded song I wrote for some friends who were enrolled with Teen Challenge. I believe it's biblically applicable for every Christian.

> Don't let the world quench the fire I've ignited.
> It burns in your soul; let it turn into gold.
> Don't let the world steal the joy I've provided.
> It's not of this earth, but neither are you.

> *My Spirit will never let you go.*
> *My love stretches far beyond your darkest road;*
> *It will reach to the depths of hell for you.*
> *My cross is the anchor holding you.*

> Don't let the world take the peace I have planted.
> Let it grow in your heart. Keep trusting in me.
> Don't let despair as a spirit overcome you.
> You are seated here with me. I will keep you free.

My mind has not changed. My heart is still the same.
As the day I took those nails for you.
I won't turn my face away. I'll not forget your name.
I'll complete the work I started in you.

Wonder upon wonder. Grace upon grace. Love everlasting. God is awesome, we are to be like him.

6. Ticket to Ride

When I first read the life stories of David Wilkerson,[1] Jackie Pullinger,[2] John Wesley,[3] George Mueller,[4] Rees Howells[5] and Smith Wigglesworth,[6] I was awed. As a young Christian, I would dream about their exploits with God, but I didn't know God's ways. I didn't know what to expect from him. Are these people the chosen few, or can anybody live an awesome life? My question was, 'Lord, do I have the green light?'

I used to ask my Christian friends, but I never got a clear answer. Maybe they were judging me according to the flesh; I don't know. Back then, they were probably asking themselves, 'Can God actually use redeemed hippies? Can anything good come out of Woodstock? I mean, look at him. Where's his tie? Why does he live in a tepee and not a house? Why doesn't he buy a new pair of shoes instead of using duct tape to keep the sole from flapping?'

My soul was stirred, but not the one hanging on my foot. I was hungry for God. I loved Jesus Christ. I wanted to run and not walk. I wanted to please the One who had delivered me from my drug addiction and hopeless life. I wanted to follow, but I didn't know what to expect or how far I could go before God said: 'Far enough, hippie. That's not for you. Go take a bath and get a haircut.' Ouch! Fortunately, God never said that to me.[7]

I was especially intrigued by an incident in the life of Rees Howells.[8] He had to get to London, but he didn't have any money for the trip. His faith led him to the train station, but then what? As he stood there, the Holy Spirit asked him what he would do if he had the money. Rees said he would get in the queue (the line) and wait for his turn to purchase the ticket. God then instructed him to do it.

So, like the dozen people in front of him, Rees stepped up and waited his turn. He winced as they dug into their wallets and purses. Rees couldn't do that. As in the old cartoons I used to watch, moths would be flying out of his pockets. His resources were not of this world.

He had no idea how this was going to pan out. He had oil in his lamp but no cash in the bank. The devil's taunts grew louder as he neared the counter. The heckling in his head was real, and the pressure was on, but Rees kept steady and on course. He reminded himself of God's faithfulness and his promises. Rees didn't believe God would leave him stranded. This is what faith looks like. We often confess faith in the abstract but, as James said, 'Faith by itself, if it is not accompanied by action, is dead.'[9]

With only two people in front of him, Rees inched towards the counter, wondering how all this was going to play out. Is this faith or folly? If the sea was going to split, now would be a good time. That's when someone stepped out of the crowd and put thirty shillings into Rees's hand. The sea had parted, and Rees was walking through on dry land. He joyfully purchased his ticket, just like everyone else in line, but his was provided by his heavenly Father.

This was Rees's Red Sea crossing, and he never forgot it. The miracle, though, was not just the provision; it was the whole process. One, God actually spoke to Rees. Two, Rees heard and recognized this otherworldly voice. Three, Rees took the risk and obeyed, not knowing the outcome. Rees was squeezing into a world he could not see with his own eyes. That day was awesome. This is what the adventure-driven life looks like.

After reading this story, I was up for the divine venture, so I planned to follow Rees's example. I would take the train from Colorado to visit my mom. I would go and stand in line, and God would lead someone to come up and give me money before I got to the counter. I mean, isn't this the way Christians are supposed to travel? We travel by faith, not by sight or pre-booked tickets. Yee-haw!

A few days before my departure, I was talking to my pastor. I told him about my faith-filled plan. He just looked at me as if I was on something. Our conversation was blunt and short-lived.

'Richard, do you have the money for a ticket?'

'Yes.'

'Then go and buy a ticket.'

That was it, and I did. Rees Howells needed a miracle; I already had the money. Somehow, I didn't feel very awesome that day. I was just like everyone else in that train station. I felt about as awesome as my friend's cheeseburger but still, something triggered in me to see God's hand at work in miraculous ways. Can we be as awesome as the people we read about? God, is the adventure of an awesome life just for the chosen few, or is it for me and all your followers? I wonder.

As my Bible knowledge and Holy Spirit encounters increase, I'm learning that the only one holding me back from a godly, miracle-filled, adventurous, holy, awesome life is me. Jesus set us free without an agenda. He set us free so we could choose the direction of our lives. He set us free so we could fulfil that destiny. He liberated us for freedom's sake. Sin, Satan and this world no longer rule over us. That 'high hand' has been severed. It is the gift of God. 'It is for freedom that Christ has set us free' (Gal. 5:1). The green light is on. It's a go!

We choose how deep we want to dive with Jesus. We determine the height we will climb with him. We decide to follow Jesus on the water or remain seated in the boat. If we want more Holy Spirit adventure, Jesus beckons: 'Step out in faith. Bring it on. I'm ready.'

> The eyes of the LORD search the whole earth in order to strengthen those whose hearts are fully committed to him.
>
> *(2 Chr. 16:9, NLT)*

> Call to me and I will answer you and tell you great and unsearchable things you do not know.
>
> *(Jer. 33:3)*

> Very truly I tell you, whoever believes in me will do the works I have been doing, and they will do even greater things than these, because I am going to the Father.
>
> *(John 14:12)*[1]

God doesn't restrict our lives; he enhances them. Why wouldn't he? His Holy Spirit rules in our hearts and minds. God commanded the fire to burn on the altar and never go out.[2] He is not into mediocrity, but he sure loves godly desire and passion.[3] He loves to see greater faith at work and to honour it.[4] Jesus is ready to take it to the next level with us. This is the way he lived, and we are to be like him.

If we want adventure like the people we read about, then we have to believe as they believed, seek as they sought, obey as they obeyed, sacrifice as they sacrificed, pray with the same fervency, and worship. The only one holding us back from a life filled with godly awe is ourselves. If we want more of God, we have to make more room for him in our lives.

There is no one more equipped to live an awesome life, day by day, than the obedient follower of Jesus Christ. God withholds nothing from us. The table is set. The feast is ready. The invitation has been sent. The sacrifice is served. The Holy Spirit is in us. We manifest the gifts and the fruit of the Holy Spirit. We carry this treasure in our mortal bodies.

> He who did not spare his own Son, but gave him up for us all – how will he not also, along with him, graciously give us all things?
>
> *(Rom. 8:32)*

> But we have this treasure in jars of clay *to show* that this all-surpassing power is *from God and not from us.*
>
> *(2 Cor. 4:7, italics mine)*

> Praise be to the God and Father of our Lord Jesus Christ, who has blessed us in the heavenly realms with *every spiritual blessing* in Christ.
>
> *(Eph. 1:3, italics mine)*

His divine power has given us everything we need for a godly life through our knowledge of him who called us by his own glory and goodness.

(2 Pet. 1:3)

Moses enters the tent to hear the voice of God; the Hebrews stand outside, restricting themselves to the voice of Moses. Rahab, in faith, stands as a solitary figure, protecting the messengers of God in a town crying out for blood. While Saul's army is laying down its sword, David is picking up stones for his slingshot. Peter unexpectedly jumps out of the boat while the others sit stunned.

Like Moses, we are called to listen to the voice of God. Like Rahab, we are called to faithfully stand in the face of life-threatening opposition. Like David, we are called to boldly use whatever he has put in our hands. Like Peter, we are called to follow Jesus wherever he may take us. Isn't this the way a Christian lives? These people were stepping into the adventure. They were awesome. They listened and followed their faith in God. God is calling us to champion what he has set before us, not to passively wait for someone else to take our place (where's the adventure in that?). If we stopped at the red light, it wasn't God who put it there.

8. Clocks and Watches

For years, I co-pastored in Belfast, Northern Ireland. The church hired a company to paint the inside of the building. Shortly after they started, I introduced myself to them. I had the freedom to tell them what God had done for me and about Jesus Christ. Later that evening, when I returned home, I had this conversation with my wife.

'Richard, I was chatting with the painters today, and they said you had spoken to them.'

'Yeah, I enjoyed the conversation. They seem like good guys.'

'They also said it was a bit weird meeting you.'

'Really! That's cool. In what way?'

'They said the clock behind you on the wall stopped ticking when you spoke to them. They assumed it had something to do with God, the church and you being there talking to them about Jesus. They thought it was kind of spooky and supernatural.'

'Wow, that's quite a leap from a dead clock to a divine encounter. Tomorrow, I'll go and change the battery.'

I'm learning that God has inscrutable ways to speak to us. The next day, before the painters arrived, I bought a battery and put it in the clock. The peculiar thing was that when I turned the clock over to reset the hands, it was already pointing at the right time. I thought, 'What are the odds of that?' I felt God was saying, 'Pay attention.'

Two weeks later, when the job was finished, the foreman came to the evening service. As a church, we wanted to thank and honour him and his team publicly for the fine work they had done. While we were saying goodbye, I mentioned what my wife told me about the stopped clock and then changing the battery to discover the clock was already strangely set to the right time. I felt that the Creator's fingerprints were all over this, so I told him, 'God is speaking to you, Thomas. He's wanting you to know he sees you, and he's revealing himself. He's calling you, kind of like he called Moses to the burning bush.'

The foreman just looked at me as though I were on a different planet – he may be right. Then, jokingly, I said, 'If you don't acknowledge him, he'll probably stop your watch just to get your attention.'

He didn't smile at that; he just looked at his wrist. Amazement filled his face as he exclaimed, 'Whoa, he did! God just stopped my watch!' He showed it to me to confirm that he wasn't playing around or going crazy.

What could I say? Another battery glitch? I don't think so. God was in this whole clock/watch scenario, and it was fascinating to follow it through. Signs and wonders were lapping on the shore of our church and it was awesome.

I told him again, 'God loves you, Thomas. He's calling out to you, my friend. He's saying it's time to get real, it's time to meet with him.'

That's when the painter quickly stepped through the door and exited into the night. However, a few months later, he returned and asked if I would officiate at the renewal of his wedding vows to his wife. It was an honour. God is still at work.

There's no way I could have orchestrated any of this. I just went along for the ride that God was taking me on. The whole episode was unconventionally awesome. As a matter of fact, incidents like this happen all the time. It's as though God is following us around, saying, in my case, 'Heh, Richard, let's have some fun today.' So I follow.

Uber Encounter

In April 2017, I had the privilege of attending a church leaders' conference in Redding, California. A small group of us went to town for lunch during one of the breaks. After the meal, Paul, our friend and driver, said he had to go, but he ordered us an Uber to take us back to the conference. He said to look for a black Honda, and the driver's name is José. The sad thing is, I'd never heard of an Uber. I had no idea what it was. So I presumed José was one of Paul's friends who was doing us a kind favour. I was wrong. Paul had never met José. The service told Paul the driver's name so we wouldn't jump into the wrong car – done that before.

Well, before long, our ride pulls up, and the driver introduces himself as José. So far, so good. I jumped in the front seat, and my two friends settled in the back. In my blissful ignorance, I had this conversation with the driver on the way to church.

'Howdy, José! Thank you for picking us up and taking us back to the church. It's very kind. How do you know Paul?'

'What? I don't know any Paul. What are you talking about?'

'You know, Paul. Where did you first meet him?'

'I don't know Paul! Are you talking about the Bible? I read some things about Paul in the Bible.'

'Oh, that's good. Are you a Christian man?'

'I sometimes pray, and wonder about God, but I have a lot of questions.'

Now, as you can imagine, my friends in the back seat were chuckling all the way to church. I didn't know why they were laughing, but sometimes ignorance really is bliss. After I had answered a few of José's questions, we pulled up to the building. Our chat ends like this.

'I know this place. I've dropped people off here before.'

'Have you ever been inside for one of the services? I'm sure you'd find answers to a lot of your questions and even meet God here.'

'Does it cost anything?'

'No, it's free, and everyone would welcome you as a friend. It's a great place to be.'

'What time does it start on Sunday?'

'Different times, but there's a service at 10:30.'

'Yeah, thank you. I'll come this Sunday.'

We said goodbye, and he drove away. My two friends were laughing more than ever now. Later, I discovered what an Uber was and how bizarre the conversation with José must have been. I just marked it up as another embarrassing but enlightening moment. Does this story register anywhere on the awesome scale? I think so.

I hope we are all beginning to realize that the call to be awesome isn't about us and our selfies and how great we think we are – because we aren't that great. It's God who is awesome; we're just a reflection made in his image. The call to be awesome every day is dependent on him, not on us. All we do is let God be awesome through us. Let him shine. It's not about me and my ego quest. If we continue to live in the tangible presence of the Almighty, he watches our back. He'll even be awesome among us, the world's weak and foolish, glorifying himself through our most embarrassing moments. That's what makes the adventure, the life with God, fun, humbling and so alive.

PART TWO

TWO

The

Wardrobe

Why would any Bible reader presume that an awesome life before an awesome God is impossible this side of eternity? It's probably because deep down we think it's unattainable – we can't do it. We don't have the will, the strength, or the wisdom and knowledge to see it through. We know we are saved by faith and not by works, but that usually doesn't stop us from trying. It's still a challenge to resist self-effort. In our own strength, it is impossible, but God never intended us to live the Christian life in our own strength. That's like putting on a mask. It may look spiritually authentic on the outside, but inwardly, it just doesn't produce fruit.

> You know we never used flattery, nor did we put on a mask to cover up greed – God is our witness.
>
> *(1 Thess. 2:5)*

Do you have a wardrobe full of masks and behaviours you desire but have a hard time acquiring? We silently carry a list of biblical attributes we want to activate in our lives. We read about the fruit of the Holy Spirit: love, joy, peace, patience, kindness, goodness, faithfulness, gentleness, and self-control.[1] It's difficult to be awesome without the fruit and gifts of the Holy Spirit made alive in and through us. We know that many of these attributes don't come easily or naturally, but we still try to produce them ourselves, or at least make a good show that we possess them.

The Bible tells me to be patient and self-controlled, so today I will be a model of patience and self-control. I vow not to threaten or yell at anyone who annoys me. I will not stamp their head with the stapler or gouge their eye out with a spoon. I am a Christian, and I will act like one!

So, we go to our closet and pull out the mask labelled 'patience'. How hard can it be? We slap it on our faces and go out the door smiling like Ned Flanders.[2] The first ten minutes go well. We pat ourselves on the back. Then someone pulls out in front of us. It's a clunker. It crawls down the road, sticking to the fast lane. Our inner dialogue goes viral. 'I don't care if it is your granny, if my dash board had a smite button, she would have been smitten back at junction 51.' It appears my 'patience' mask is starting to slip.

I patiently sit at my desk watching the clock. Bill keeps asking me stupid questions and won't leave me alone. I try to keep my mask on straight, but there's another 'smite' shouting from my heart. I'm conflicted. I need a bigger, better mask and more willpower.

The boss is in a bad mood and takes it out on the office. Inside, the smite trigger goes off like a double-barrelled shotgun. My mask starts to melt off my face. I can feel the wax running down my chin. The Flanders smile becomes a sneer. My eyes are watering, not because I'm sorrowful or repentant; I'm just fighting the urge to punch my boss in the face and wallop a staple into Bill's forehead.

At the end of the day, I drive home. I was not awesome. I wasn't behaving like Jesus. I lost my holiness badge back at junction 12. I pull into the driveway. At last, I am home. My mask is in tatters. All the other masks in the closet mock me as I walk through the front door: 'Loser, loser, and you call yourself a Christian?'

What can I say? 'Lord, I have failed again! I am not patient, loving, or kind. My mind is not filled with godly thoughts or whispers of grace. But, heh! I'll fix the mask and give it another go tomorrow. Amen.'

This merry-go-round is not a biblical model, and it's doomed to fail. Many are stuck here. We polish the masks and keep wearing them, thinking this is a holy and righteous thing to do, but it's a sham. With the best intentions, we wear the same masks to church. They become our public image, but it's just a façade. God is not interested in us trying to live up to his ideal because he knows we can't do it.

'But, Lord, what am I to do with all these masks? I've been collecting them for years. Aren't they biblical? Isn't this the normal Christian life? Try to be good, be wholesome, stay pure, and travel the world doing good deeds?'

'Yes, my child, but not the way you're going about it. The first thing you have to do, if you really want to live a holy, awesome life, is torch the closet. Use a flame-thrower and destroy the masks. If you don't, you'll never walk the path I've laid out for you. I've called you to be real and authentic – not a caricature of me, but a clear image of who I am and what I am like. Quit striving and enter into my rest.'[3]

Put It On

Now, you may be thinking torching the masks was a bad idea. No one likes an empty closet. What are we going to wear? We feel vulnerable and spiritually naked. Where's the glory? How can we be awesome without fervent participation and self-effort?[1]

These questions are logical, but the Apostle Paul tells us to change the way we think.[2] We are in a different kingdom now, and we don't play by the old rules. Worldly human effort will fail us just like the masks in the closet did.

> Are you so foolish? After beginning by means of the Spirit, are you now trying to finish by means of the flesh?
>
> *(Gal. 3:3)*

It is a step of faith to torch the masks but, surprisingly, we aren't left with a burnt-out shell. We just make room for greater possibilities. The masks are gone, but the closet is far from empty. We just couldn't see it before we lifted the flame-thrower.[3]

What's left on the hangers is born of the Spirit and can only be worn in faith. Look closely. There is a full set of armour given by God. We're instructed to put it on.[4] There's the new self, created in the divine image. We're told to put it on.[5] But more importantly, there is Christ.

Let us put aside the deeds of darkness and put on the armour of light . . . Clothe yourselves with the Lord Jesus Christ, and do not think about how to gratify the desires of the flesh.

(Rom. 13:12–14)

This new wardrobe is activated by faith. It has nothing to do with mimicry, self-effort or staging a caricature of Jesus. It's the Son of God actually living his life in and through us. This is what the Bible means when it instructs us to put on Christ. It is a deliberate act of faith, not a human display of charity or individual willpower.

I have been crucified with Christ and I no longer live, but *Christ lives in me. The life I now live in the body, I live by faith in the Son of God,* who loved me and gave himself for me.

(Gal. 2:20, italics mine)

By faith, Christ lives his life in me. Paul was not trying to live the Christian life; he was letting Christ live that life in and through him. He was not trying to be good; his faith was in the indwelling goodness of God.

Consider this. We don't possess the fruit of the Spirit because it's not ours; it belongs to the Holy Spirit. We do not possess the gifts[6] of the Spirit because they aren't ours to possess; they too belong to the Holy Spirit. We host the Holy Spirit; all that follows is grace bestowed but not owned.

I don't own God. I don't own Jesus. I don't own God's Spirit. I don't own my salvation. I don't own my place in heaven.

I don't own eternal life, the gifts, the fruit or the divine nature. As Christians, we host a holy, otherworldly guest. God lives in us and is transforming us, but we don't own him. God the Father, the Son and Holy Spirit own us.[7]

Transformation is not independent or detached from the perpetual presence of God. Even eternal life is the life of God, his eternal presence in us. We don't own eternal life. God does. Outside of him, it doesn't exist. No one owns or has it except God alone.

> But if Christ is in you, then even though your body is subject to death because of sin, *the Spirit gives life* because of righteousness. And if the Spirit of him who raised Jesus from the dead is *living in you*, he who raised Christ from the dead will also give life to your mortal bodies *because of his Spirit who lives in you.*
>
> (Rom. 8:10–11, italics mine)

This is why Jesus said, 'Apart from me, you can do nothing.'[8] It's why he declared, 'I am the way, the truth, and the life.'[9] God may hand us a map called the Bible, but the person of Jesus is the Word,[10] and he's also the road that leads us to our final destination. It's an ongoing relationship – not just an acquiescence to a divine contract.

An awesome life requires the acknowledged, faith-aware presence of God. We have to stay close and connected, or we will wither and die. He won't desert us, but at times we drift.[11] It's imperative that we put on Christ every day. Our trust is in him, not in our ability to manifest the gifts; not in our attempts to walk in the fruit of the Spirit; not in our calling, or even in our ability to be patient and loving. I can do all things through Christ; I can do nothing without him.[12] It's grace bestowed but not owned. He lives in me, but I have to put him on every day.

Jesus didn't hand us the Bible and tell us to go out there and give it our best shot; instead, he gifted us with the Holy Spirit. We listen, and we follow. So many times, we put faith in our faith to produce his work, but this is not the well that God called us to drink from – it's not about us. I don't trust myself to follow, but I trust him to lead. I don't struggle to hear his voice; my faith is in his ability to communicate. I trust his guidance, not my acumen to suss out his will for my life. I don't even trust myself to do good deeds, but I put my faith in his compassion to move and motivate me in that direction.[13]

I often find that when I pray in the morning, my wife comes to mind. That's when I thank God for her and pray for her. Then one morning I realized that the closer I get to God and the more I dwell in God's presence, the more I love my wife. The source of love is not in me; it comes from God through me. If we find our love and patience waning, we need to look at our relationship with Jesus, not our human attempts to manifest the fruit. We are not the source.

Words One Should Never Say to the One They Love. Now that would be a first-rate title for a book. I would buy it, but heh, I could write the thing. I have blundered through many conversations. Obviously, I'm still on a learning curve when it comes to wooing and blissful domesticity.

Once, my wife prepared a special meal for me and our two boys, who were home for the holidays. I'm busy writing in my Command Centre when I hear the shout, 'Dad, dinner's ready.' I rumble down the stairs, look at the spread on the table, and announce, 'Smells great. Let's eat and get it over with.' Thankfully, the love of God and the fruit of the Holy Spirit helped us through that one.

A few years ago, my wife and I were sitting in the car, waiting for someone to open the church. I had forgotten to bring the keys. That was no biggie. We are patient that way, but what stirred the hornets' nest was when I romantically looked over and whispered, 'Let's hold hands and pretend we're still in love.'

Sometimes my sense of humour is a bit warped and untested. However, I'm learning there are some things you don't say, even in jest. Pay attention. The word 'pretend' should never leave our lips in the wooing process. It just doesn't bode well.

One morning, in response to the words, 'I love you, Richard', I muttered back, 'Ditto, babe.' Yikes! That one also entered the annals of restricted dialogue.

So, there we were, together again, sitting in a restaurant, scanning the menu. When the waitress came to our table, I found myself drawn to her and overwhelmed with love. It was the kind of affection a father has for his daughter. I couldn't shake it throughout the meal. Eventually, I said to my wife, 'I have a deep love stirring in my heart for that waitress, and I need to talk to her.' My wife didn't even flinch this time. She was used to the adventure and could sense the fingerprint of God on it, but where was the waitress? She was gone.

As we left the building, we decided to look for her in the back alley. She might be taking a break. We followed the smoke and found her outside the back door, holding a cigarette. I've discovered in awkward moments like this not to pre-think what I say but just to tell it like it is. So I blurted it out.

> I know this will sound odd but, throughout our meal, I sensed a deep love for you. Please don't panic; I'm a pastor down the road, and I find that when I sense love like this for a stranger, it's God speaking. I believe he just wants you to know he sees you. He's aware of what you are going through, and he loves you more than you realize, and he will help you. Talk to him. He wants to talk to you.

She didn't say a word. I watched as her eyes filled with tears; then came the sobs. It was convulsive. I remained silent, quietly praying, 'Now what, Lord?'

Then this thought came to me, so I asked, 'Are you into self-harm?'

She looked up and exclaimed, 'How did you know?'

Again, I told her, 'God sees you. He knows you, and he loves you deeply. He wants to help and guide you through your life.'

She gratefully let my wife and me pray with her before going back to work; her break was over. A few days later, I received an envelope. I opened a small card that simply read: 'Thank you! from Hannah, your waitress down the road'.

To me, that whole encounter was awesome. I didn't get a chance to talk to her directly about salvation, but someone will. I still pray for her. At least, we were able to encourage her on the journey. As Jesus said, 'One sows and another reaps' (John 4:37).

Had I just put on the 'love' mask, this encounter would never have happened, but when we put on Christ, things like this happen all the time. Why? Because God has been released in us. Our faith is in him to love through us, not in our attempt to stir up love or the other fruit and gifts of the Holy Spirit.[1] Put on Christ. Who knows what he has in mind for each day? That's what makes the adventure fun and unpredictable. I'm often awed by his love, his ways and his goodness.

Have you ever tried to slip a pair of jeans over your pyjamas? It's difficult to be awesome when we continue to wear the garments of earth. They don't fit us anymore. I'm not talking about cotton shirts and designer dresses; I'm speaking of spiritual deportment. Since birth, we have been assimilated and clothed by the gods of this world. These garments are no longer adequate. We have outgrown them. By faith, we are called to rip them from our hearts. If we don't, we'll end up confessing the name but not living the life. That is not awesome. It's a Christian tragedy.

> You were taught, with regard to your former way of life, to *put off your old self*, which is being corrupted by its deceitful desires; to be made new in the attitude of your minds; and to put on the new self, created to be like God in *true* righteousness and holiness.
>
> (Eph. 4:22–4, italics mine)

The moment we draw our first breath, Mother Earth is there, clothing us with the values of this broken world. As we grow, we try to break free, but no matter how radical or avant-garde our lifestyle, we are still assimilated into a system.

I look at bikers and see the patches on their leather jackets; some are disturbing, some are really cool. I know some bikers who would shake my hand and others who would break it. I must admit, though, that I can see the attraction of charging

down Route 66 on a Harley with a gang of like-minded en-
thusiasts. I can imagine wearing a Viking helmet with a 3-foot
beard flapping in the wind as I speed past a family car and
spit a wad of tobacco on their windshield. Wild and free – yet
utterly assimilated.

There was no difficulty recognizing hippies back in the sixties and early seventies. Beads, long hair, tie-dyed dresses and
shirts, smelling of pot, flashing the peace sign, and getting
high. Those were the days: peace, love and rock 'n' roll, Woodstock, Haight Ashbury, Greenwich Village; and the Summer
of Love. It all came in one big package. You were either in or
out, cool or straight, hippie or redneck, socking it to the man,
or you were the man. Again, we thought we were wild and
free, independent of the system, breaking loose from social
restrictions, but we too were wholly assimilated.

Consider the Goths, with their bleached faces, jet-black
hair, deathrock, and screaming skulls. It's another subculture
that shouts against civil expectations. Then we have the hip-
sters and skinny jeans; the hackers bonded to illicit keystrokes;
the swastikas spewing hatred and anarchy; the gamers lost in a
virtual world of nerd-dom. The unending list drills deeper and
deeper into the human psyche. The individual's heart wants to
break free but, with each step, we find ourselves exchanging
one chain for another, trapped and constricted – assimilated.

This world, with all its challenges, pains, joys, fears, and
confusion, is the realm we navigate. It's big and messy and offers innumerable roads and caves to crawl into. It's where we
draw our sustenance, our identity, our purpose and our pleas-
ures. It's the only playground available to us. There is no other.
I once asked my 12-year-old son about his goal in life. Without

flinching, he said, 'World domination!' Hmm, that sounds like assimilation to me, and he doesn't even have a job yet.

From the moment our head is laid in the crib, the world, the flesh, and the devil whisper, 'You will be assimilated like all the rest of them. There is no escape.'[1] We are born slaves to sin, slaves to our education, and slaves to our culture: this world's values, history, language, sliding morality and incessant philosophies. We try to resist and fight the world, but it's impossible. We've been integrated without recourse. So we search for help and direction from anyone who functions outside the system. Some people are drawn to counter-cultural mavericks living off the grid. Others step into the nearest cul-de-sac that attracts them. We all identify with some group or tribe. For many, it doesn't take long to realize we are still in the world, and it has fallen. So we look up.

> As the heavens are higher than the earth,
>> so are my ways higher than your ways
>> and my thoughts than your thoughts.

(Isa. 55:9)

This is the One many of us eventually call out to: the One who dwells completely outside. We need this 'other' to release our chains and set us free. So God Almighty keeps breaking into our world and is constantly fishing. He casts his line, and anyone who will bite he reels to himself and unshackles them.

> For as high as the heavens are above the earth,
>> so great is his love for those who fear him.

(Ps. 103:11)

We will never be awesome as long as we are assimilated and conformed to the world's system. The old garments were fashioned by the gods of the earth. They are hand-me-downs from a broken loom. As Christians, we are called to strip them off because they don't display the label of heaven. We must discard the old so we can put on the new. This doesn't necessarily mean we have to abandon our tribe. There are many Christian bikers, Goths, and clandestine hippies. We just work with God to redeem our tribe from the inside out. This is the way God works with us. People don't need a re-imaged lifestyle; they need to see and embrace the divine alternative.

A neighbour once addressed me as 'a man of the cloth'. That was cool since I wear only jeans and shirts from local department stores. This idiom is often applied to clergy, whether they wear vestments or not. I do find it interesting, though, how society puts the emphasis on the garment and not the vocation. The Coptic martyrs in present-day Egypt are referred to as the 'people of the cross'.[1] If we could choose, I think most of us would rather be called a man or a woman of the cross than a man or a woman of the cloth. However, biblically speaking, there is more to this idea than we realize.

> People brought all who were ill to him and begged him to let those who were ill just touch the edge of his cloak, and all who touched it were healed.
>
> *(Matt. 14:35–6)*

> God did extraordinary miracles through Paul, so that even handkerchiefs and aprons that had touched him were taken to those who were ill, and their illnesses were cured and the evil spirits left them.
>
> *(Acts 19:11–12)*

> Just then a woman who had been subject to bleeding for twelve years came up behind him and touched the edge of his cloak. She said to herself, 'If I only touch his cloak, I will be healed.'
>
> *(Matt. 9:20–21)*

I often wondered why this woman wanted to touch the cloak of Jesus. Did she think the chances of touching him physically were hit-or-miss because of her proximity? Did she assume her reach wouldn't stretch far enough because of the jostling crowd? From our contemporary, Western mindset, this is what we often assume – but it's not correct. It had nothing to do with expediency, but she was driven by a focused determination. The garment was the desired target. She knew Jesus was literally a man of the cloth, and his garment was the incentive for her resolve. To her, the edge of his cloak was the bull's-eye. Why? Because in the ancient Near East, clothing was more than just a garment to cover the body; it was an extension of who you were, your position, your personhood, your anointing and your authority in the community.[2]

Consider the saga of Elijah and Elisha. Elisha asks for a double portion of Elijah's spirit.[3] Through the story, Elisha receives two garments from Elijah, symbolizing the double portion.[4] Elisha then takes the second garment and parts the Jordan River with it, just as Elijah did earlier in the text.[5] The anointing extended to the garment.

In the ancient Near East the hem of the robe carried the same weight and authority as a signature does today.[6] Tablets from the early city-state of Mari[7] inform us that the edge of a garment was often pressed into a clay tablet to ratify legal contracts.[8] The prophets beyond Israel would cut off the edge of their cloak and post it with their message to authenticate the oracle. During a divorce, the husband would cut off the hem of a wife's garment to signify the separation.[9] This is why King David's conscience bothered him when he cut off the edge of Saul's robe; he had symbolically mugged God's anointed.[10] God chose the king, and to raise your hand against him (even against the garment he was wearing) was to raise your hand against the one who called him – not a good idea.

Biblically, the putting on and discarding of clothes also functions as a prophetic backdrop to enhance the storyline. It's a fascinating subject for those who want to delve deeper into the Bible narrative. As you read, pay attention to the use of clothing. You will discover that when people are about to lose their status, they often lose a garment. When people are about to be promoted, they receive a garment, or something equivalent, to put on.

Consider the life of Joseph. Whenever he is elevated, he receives clothing; when he's about to lose his status, a garment is taken from him.[11] The tale of Potiphar's wife is a good illustration. 'One day he went into the house to attend to his duties, and none of the household servants was inside. She caught him by his cloak and said, "Come to bed with me!" But he left his cloak in her hand and ran out of the house' (Gen. 39:11–12). This is prior to the police arriving and tossing him into prison.

The same is true in the lives of King Saul and David.[12] Throughout David's rise to the throne, David continually gains apparel, weapons, and armour, while Saul and his son Jonathan discard and lose both their armour and their clothing.[13]

> So Saul went to Naioth at Ramah. But the Spirit of God came even on him, and he walked along prophesying until he came to Naioth. He stripped off his garments, and he too prophesied in Samuel's presence. He lay naked all that day and all that night.
>
> *(1 Sam. 19:23–4)*

This passage often confuses people. Why did God allow a man like Saul to prophesy with the prophets? Why doesn't the text record his oracles? It's because the original audience wouldn't need the words to know the significance of the event. Saul's nakedness was the point. It was a prophetic enactment of his future. He will be stripped of his anointing, royal authority, power and kingship.[14]

The act of putting on and taking off clothes, or even tearing them,[15] has far more significance than the actual deed. When the Bible speaks of putting on and taking off as a metaphor or metaphysical act, it is no less a reality than if you actually button your shirt or pull up your trousers. To put on Christ is to walk in the anointing of the Holy Spirit.

15. Twilight Zone

I never experienced an ego boost standing naked in front of a full-length mirror. The narcissist may smile and wish they could go through life wearing Speedos or some other swimming attire, but not me. As a matter of fact, I have had a few body-exposure nightmares, and they aren't pleasant. There's nothing more disconcerting than standing in the hub of a busy mall and realizing you forgot to put on your clothes – big yikes! I was relieved when I woke up. Do you think this dream would bother Arnie Schwarzenegger?

Now, I'm not going to bring Freud into this conversation, but I will invite God. We've already seen that the Bible has a lot to say about clothing, what we put on and take off – but then there is also that middle place – that space between darkness and light. Rod Serling calls it the *Twilight Zone*.[1] The Scriptures call it 'nakedness' or being 'unclothed'.[2] The only positive statement about nakedness in the Bible is just before Adam and Eve commit the crime.[3]

Scripturally, nakedness was far more serious than the embarrassing exposure of our bodies. It signified vulnerability, no position,[4] no status, defeat,[5] a loss of dignity,[6] an absence of power,[7] and at times, it indicated the loss of God's anointing.[8] Job said, 'Naked I came from my mother's womb, and naked I shall depart'[9] but hopefully we won't find ourselves exposed in the mall before our time is up.[10]

The Apostle Paul tells us things we should take off, and what we should put on, but he never leaves us in the twilight zone, because it's a dangerous and vulnerable place to be. God put clothes on Adam and Eve.[11] The prodigal son was reclothed by his father.[12] Paul tells us we are to put off our old selves, but don't stand there vulnerable and naked; 'Put on the new self, created to be like God in true righteousness and holiness.'[13] Jesus explains what often happens to those who take something off but hang out in the twilight zone and put nothing on in its place.[14]

> When an impure spirit comes out of a person, it goes through arid places seeking rest and does not find it. Then it says, 'I will return to the house I left.' When it arrives, it finds the house unoccupied, swept clean and put in order. Then it goes and takes with it seven other spirits more wicked than itself, and they go in and live there. And the final condition of that person is worse than the first.
>
> *(Matt. 12:43–5)*

It's just not wise to leave your house empty, or yourself naked. According to science, the physical world abhors a vacuum, but so does life in the Spirit. The spiritual realm will take advantage of our exposure and vulnerability. This is why Paul tells us to put on the full armour of God.[15] The physical world is a force to be reckoned with, but so is the world of the spirit. Don't face the day or the battle naked and unarmed. There is too much at stake.

For many, the month of February is the graveyard of good intentions. It's where we bury our New Year's resolutions. 'Here lies my objective for 2023: rest in peace. Yee-haw, pass the ice cream and chocolate fudge brownies, and don't forget the whipped cream!'

We often crash and burn because our goal is to strip off and face the coming year naked. I'm going to give up smoking. I'm going to quit swearing. I'm going to stop eating doughnuts. I'm going to lose a hundred pounds – but this is only half the process. Perhaps our next New Year's resolution should focus more on what we are going to put on in its place than what we hope to take off.

I was the associate pastor in Glasgow for four years and also served with Teen Challenge. We had a renovated bus to meet people suffering from addictions. We offered them a safe, neutral place with food, drink, and a space to talk and pray. Many who came on board often told the same story: 'I locked myself in a room for a few days to kick the habit; but when I left the room, I started up again.'

The failure wasn't in their desire to live drug-free; the collapse was their lack of follow-through. What were they going to put in its place? They left themselves naked and vulnerable. We were never meant to settle down in the twilight world of exposure. We should get out of there as quickly as we can, but we need somewhere to go. This was something many of the addicts didn't have, so the spirit returned and resettled in the empty house. This is how I explained it to them.

> Your whole life revolves around your drug habit and its thrills. You get the excitement of going into stores and shop-lifting to get money for the next purchase. Then there's the covert adventure with the dealer who sells you the drugs. Staying out of jail is also a creative goal that holds your attention. Then, there's the needle, the preparation and the rush. You exist and survive on extreme

highs and lows. It is commendable that you want to get off this train, but you will never be free if all you do is try to quit. You have to put something in its place. You can't lay all this down and survive in a vacuum. You aren't made to live that way.

God delivered me from drugs when I first became a Christian. He gave me the power to say, 'no'. He took that curse off me. His Holy Spirit moved in, and the other spirits ran for their lives. I stayed free with continual devotion and trust in him. By the grace of God, I attended every church service and Christian event. I made drug-free friends. I read the Bible. I sought the face of God. I prayed. In faith, I put on Christ and served him on the streets and in the church. I have been free ever since. The house was not left empty. I thank God for that.

Years ago, we bought an old coach house, a wayside inn in rural Northern Ireland. It was built in 1740. We opened it up as a place of prayer. I always found it amusing when people asked if it was haunted. I would tell them, 'Yes, it's haunted by only one ghost, the Holy Ghost. We invited Jesus into our home and have been hosting God's Spirit ever since.' Our house is not empty.

Some have walked through the front door and started to cry the moment they stepped over the threshold. We had one woman fall to her knees in worship the moment she entered the little prayer chapel in the backyard. This, too, is awesome. We changed a lot of things in that house when we moved in. We took things off and put things on. It was what we put on that made all the difference.

Paul tells us to stop lying (take it off),[16] but don't just bite your tongue and remain silent; don't leave yourself vulnerable and naked. Open your mouth and face reality. Stand up for the truth.

Take off stealing, but in its place, get a job, earn some money, and give to those in need.[17] Don't let unwholesome talk or gossip come out of your mouth. Start thinking good things about people. Then speak it out. Don't remain silent. Instead, encourage others; only speak well of them. Use words that lift them up, not tear them down.

Take off bitterness, rage, and anger; brawling and slander; and every form of malice. Then, in its place, put on kindness, compassion, and forgiveness.[18] The Bible never leaves us in the twilight zone or standing naked in the middle of a mall. If the Scriptures tell us to take something off, in the same breath we're told to put something on in its place.

So what are we going to wear as we leave the house today? In the morning, as I reach into the closet, I choose to put on Christ. I read my Bible. I pray, and I listen to the voice of God. I worship and seek his presence in the Holy Spirit, and then, by faith, I exit the front door clothed with Christ. The Holy Spirit is not only in me but also let loose and unleashed upon me. I go out expecting divine encounters to honour Christ. Take off the old, put on the new, and put on Christ!

Medieval monks recruited, baptized, and discipled children at an early age. I've heard that in one monastery, the youngster would be given a robe like all the other monks, but one size fits all.[1] It was designed for adults. The child would have to tie up the sleeves and lift the hem each time they stumbled down the hallway. However, this wasn't an act of monkish humour or frugality; it illustrated the child's acceptance into the order as a full-grown brother. The trainees were honoured as fully fledged monks, but they still had a lot to learn. As they grew in body, they were also growing in faith and custom. When the robe actually fitted them, there was no dichotomy between designation and practice. This is such a great picture of life in the Spirit.

We look in our otherworldly closet, and we see the robes, the divine robes: a robe of righteousness, a robe of holiness before the Lord. God the Father deems us holy and righteous through what his Son procured for us on the cross. From the moment we believe and trust in Jesus we are unquestionably accepted and adopted into God's family. We are not on trial. Our salvation is not probationary or provisional. We are fully fledged members of the kingdom of God. We are adopted into his family with all the rights and privileges of heaven. We are entitled by the Creator of the universe – but is entitlement the end goal of salvation?

The Bible tells us we are the righteousness of Christ,[2] but we don't always do righteous deeds. This is bothersome.

The Bible says we are holy, but our thoughts and actions at times negate the premise. This is also discouraging. Entitlement without restraint or accountability does not honour God or bring him glory. We feel it when we sin. We are acutely aware when people on the street aren't drawn to Jesus as they observe our actions, responses, and behaviours. It grieves us.

> Be careful to live properly among your unbelieving neighbors. Then even if they accuse you of doing wrong, they will see your honorable behavior, and they will give honor to God when he judges the world.
>
> *(1 Pet. 2:12, NLT)*

We are saved by faith in Jesus, but what is the end goal of salvation? Entitlement? What does God get out of it? Is God just populating heaven and earth with those who wear the salvation badge but ignore the qualities it represents? 'I signed the contract, now I'm in; I'm entitled.'

We often quote, 'There is now no condemnation for those who are in Christ Jesus' (Rom. 8:1). However, it's hard to accept Paul's wonderful declaration when we still struggle not to slap a staple into Bill's forehead or smite our neighbour's granny off the road. If we read a bit further in Paul's letter, we find the statement is not as carte blanche as we often make it out to be. 'There is now no condemnation for those who are in Christ Jesus . . . who do not live according to the flesh but according to the Spirit' (Rom. 8:1–4). Hmm, there's that phrase again. It's the Holy Spirit living in and through us that connects the heart of God with our heart; not only influencing our attitudes but also motivating our behaviour.

Just like the young monks in the monastery, we are authorized and approved. We are entitled to righteousness and holiness, but these are very big robes to wear. Be holy. Be perfect in the same way God is perfect. Be like Jesus in this world. Like the young monks, the clothes of our entitlement are too large. We put them on, but we have to tie up the sleeves because we fumble with them. We are still maturing. We are God's children. We lift up the hem because we trip over it.

God the Father, Jesus and the Holy Spirit have entitled and marked us for eternal salvation, but our salvation is not what God gets out of it. His goal is that we are transformed into the image of his Son, that we are motivated by love, and that our lives reflect the love of God in everything we do.

God knows he has given us very big shoes to fill. This is why God endowed us with full entitlement – the larger-than-life garment to wrap ourselves in. The entitlement grants us access to the rights and privileges of the kingdom of God. We are his children. Without the resources of heaven, we could never grow into the garment God has placed on us. We could not achieve God's goal without them.

We make deposits as we lay up our treasures in heaven,[3] and we make withdrawals with each prayer request and obedient act of faith. The entitlement secures our account. The account is never terminated. Our entitlement guarantees this.

Like the neophyte monks, we have been given an adult robe – washed in the blood of Jesus Christ. God knows we will trip over it now and then, but it doesn't change our status. We are in the maturation process. We are growing up to be like him. On earth, we are progressing – we are in a state of becoming. Luke tells us, 'Jesus grew in wisdom and stature, and in favour with God and man.'[4] He was growing into his messianic robe and calling.

As the young monks developed in understanding and physique, they remained steady, listening to and observing their elders. They didn't throw in the towel when the task seemed too big, or they tripped now and then in the hallway. The older monks didn't discard the young because they acted like youngsters. They knew these young monks were in transition. They were all looking toward the end goal. The youngsters were growing into their robes physically and positionally, just as Jesus did in his humanity, just as we are now maturing.

The massive robe and big shoes are a constant reminder of the goal and the journey we are on. I am in training. The young monks knew they'd be mature monks one day – their robes would be a snug fit. We, too, will one day be perfected like Christ in this world, but this doesn't mean that we are stagnant, waiting for the culmination. The process is happening right now. Development is taking place at this very moment. We are growing and advancing from glory to glory. We shouldn't condemn ourselves when we trip over the hem. We just get back up and ask our dad to brush us off[5] and keep looking to the author and finisher of our faith.[6]

God is the one who began the good work in us.[7] He is the one who prunes and brings out the gold.[8] He convicts us of sin[9] and gives us the power to overcome temptation.[10] He even makes room for us when we sin, trip and fall.[11] God does his thing and we co-operate with him.

> Therefore, my dear friends, as you have always obeyed – not only in my presence, but now much more in my absence – continue to work out your salvation with fear and trembling, for it is God who works in you to will and to act in order to fulfil his good purpose.

Do everything without grumbling or arguing, so that you may become blameless and pure, 'children of God without fault in a warped and crooked generation.' Then you will shine among them like stars in the sky as you hold firmly to the word of life.

(Phil. 2:12–16)[12]

We are not the ones in control of our salvation or even our growth. God does the work, but we actively participate in it. It is a joint venture – a relationship. Theologically, it can be stated like this: justification is the robe, and sanctification is the process of growing into it, ever becoming more Christlike. One day we will wear the garment, and the garment won't wear us.

PART THREE

The Matrix

The call to be awesome is built into the matrix. Our special place in creation is crucial to its survival, but we are often too self-absorbed to appreciate what God has given and allotted to us. There's much talk about saving the planet, but our focus is on government, weather, science and technology. We are always trying to fix it ourselves, as though the Creator has nothing to do with it or us. In heaven, our independence is notorious, but God is not going to let us have the last word on anything. The good news is that God also wants to save creation and us with it.

If we want to save the planet, we have to look up and stop looking down. We are created to love God and each other. If we don't, all creation will be lost. Global warming and the depletion of the ozone layer are nothing in comparison. So when we become too enamoured with this world, God has a way of breaking in and getting our attention. It's inspired. Some fight him, try to ignore him, or even explain him away, but they won't be able to stop him. His ways with us are inscrutable, and he did something ingenious. He . . . oops, I shouldn't get ahead of myself here. Instead, let's start by turning to one of the most depressing texts in the Bible. Sometimes we find the profoundest truths buried in the most unlikely places.

Have you ever read Ecclesiastes? To be fair, it's not the first book of the Bible I turn to when I need a bit of a lift or encouragement. I would guess it's not your first choice either, but for those among us who feel a tinge of guilt due to excessive joy and happiness, read Ecclesiastes; it's a great neutralizer. It will throw you back into the arms of the world's nihilistic pessimism before you finish reading the first line.

'Meaningless! Meaningless!'
   says the Teacher.
'Utterly meaningless!
   Everything is meaningless.'

(Eccl. 1:2)

Here is where the deep voice of a radio presenter breaks in and says, 'Welcome. You have just opened Pandora's box of the Bible. Like a rollercoaster from below, get ready to slide into the abyss as we explore the despondent cynicism of human existence.' Yee-haw!

Tradition tells us this book is one of three attributed to King Solomon. The Song of Songs is said to have been written when he was a young man in love. Proverbs was written during his middle years of discovery and understanding. Ecclesiastes is the assessment of those discovery years during the throes of old age.

Surprisingly, this enigmatic text has been nipping at my heels ever since I said 'yes' to Jesus. I remember when I first visited the church I would come to call 'home'. It was a young hippie kind of community – radically saved and unconventional. I was about one year old on the spiritual calendar when I first stepped through those doors. I was teachable but spiritually naïve. I'd welcome guidance from anyone who has walked the path longer than me.

My first encounter in that congregation was a man greeting people at the entrance. After a brief introduction, he leant in and whispered, 'Richard, have you been reading the book of Ecclesiastes?'

I answered, 'Whaaa? I never heard of Ecclesiastes.'

Then he instructed me to read it every day. I figured he knew what he was talking about, so I began my first ever descent into the melancholic ramblings of Israel's ancient king. I was a good student.

The next week I returned to that church, and my encourager friend was standing there at the door a second time. He smiled and took up where we left off the previous week.

'So Richard, have you been reading the book of Ecclesiastes?'

'Yes.'

'Did you understand it?'

'No, not really.'

'What translation did you read it from?'

'The New American Standard.'

'Won't work. You have to read it in the King James Bible.'

Well, what could I say? I shot for the A but got a D, so on Monday morning I went to the Salvation Army Thrift Store and bought a King James Version for 75 cents.

> Vanity of vanities, saith the Preacher, vanity of vanities; all is vanity. What profit hath a man of all his labour which he taketh under the sun? One generation passeth away, and another generation cometh: but the earth abideth for ever.
>
> *(Eccl. 1:2–4, KJV)*

Vanity of vanities, saith, taketh, hath, passeth, cometh, abideth, what is this? Who speaketh like this? I'm an American. Shakespeare isn't my second language, but for the next seven days I faithfully ploughed through the book of Ecclesiastes in the King James Version of the Holy Bible.

That third Sunday, I sauntered up to the church door, and there he was again – the greeter was waiting for me. I knew for sure I was going to fail the drill this time because I couldn't relate to Solomon and his existential despondency. It was lost on me. I hated to admit it, but I was flunking Christianity.

'Good morning, Richard; have you been reading the book of Ecclesiastes in the King James Version?'

'Yes.'

'Did you understand it?'

'No. I understood it less this week than I did last week.'

Then he looks at my Bible and says, 'No wonder you couldn't understand it. It can't be read in just any King James Bible; it has to be a Gideon King James Bible!' Then he lifts up his copy, which he probably got from some hotel room, and waves it about like a medal of honour. You'd think he just won the celestial Olympics.

All I really gathered from those early encounters is that the title 'Christian' doesn't always equal 'sane'. As a retired pastor, I have learned over the years to be careful about who you let loose at the front door of the church; instead, try your best to steer them. Encourage them to visit the church down the road.

I confess, I have since picked up the gauntlet thrown to me by my learned friend at the door. I have accepted the challenge to conquer and understand this mysterious book called Ecclesiastes, the one best read in the Gideon King James Version of the Holy Bible. However, I also acknowledge that if I want an A, I have to cheat. I now read it in the New International Version. To all my Christlike King James brothers and sisters reading this, I humbly apologize.

The book of Ecclesiastes is the account of a grand experiment. Like a scientist of the ancient past, King Solomon set his mind to systematically search out the meaning of life. What an enterprise! Where would a person even begin? For us, let's start by looking at the credentials of the person conducting the test.[1]

Only a king of Solomon's calibre and reputation as a wise man could even begin to perform such a methodical examination of life's benefit, value and purpose. Solomon had it all. He had the power and authority to do whatever he desired. No one stood in his way. He was the king of Israel during a time of peace. He wasn't distracted by war or enemies rattling their sabres at the border. He was free to concentrate on any project of his choosing.

Solomon was the richest man on earth. He didn't just win the lottery; he owned it.[2] Silver was so common during his administration that it littered Jerusalem like pebbles on the street.[3] Throughout his 40-year reign, gold kept pouring into his coffers from the surrounding nations, along with other riches too numerous to count. Whatever he set his heart to do, he had unlimited resources to support it.

Solomon was also a celebrity. He enjoyed kudos from all the kings and queens surrounding his domain. Foreign dignitaries would travel far and wide seeking his advice and direction.[4] He was honoured and he was favoured by God and all his neighbours.

Most importantly, Solomon was the wisest person on earth. He wasn't the Einstein or the Socrates of his day; he was the culmination of them both. His wisdom was transcendent because he received it directly from God. The Almighty was watching Solomon's back and guiding his steps.

> I will give you a wise and discerning heart, so that there will never have been anyone like you, nor will there ever be. Moreover, I will give you what you have not asked for – both wealth and honour – so that in your lifetime you will have no equal among kings. And if you walk in obedience to me and keep my decrees and commands as David your father did, I will give you a long life.
>
> *(1 Kgs 3:12–14)*

The wisdom of Ecclesiastes is phenomenal. It's astounding that of all the things Solomon could be doing and achieving in his lifetime, he wants to answer that age-old question: 'What is the meaning of life?' Now, that's what a person does with real wisdom.

The first thing Solomon sets before us is the human predicament.[5] Everything is meaningless. Nothing changes. The monotony drives him crazy. There is nothing new, and we all keep falling into the same pattern of expectation and behaviour as cognizant human beings. Our parents fought for and wanted the same things we fight for and desire. Our grandparents before them were the same. Nothing lasts, and then we die. So what's the point?

> I, the Teacher, was king over Israel in Jerusalem. I applied my mind to study and to explore by wisdom all that is done under the heavens. What a heavy burden God has laid on mankind! I

have seen all the things that are done under the sun; all of them are meaningless, a chasing after the wind.

(Eccl. 1:12–14)

That's a bit cheerless, but now for the fun part. Solomon decides the best way to conduct his experiment is to jump feet first into a lifestyle people only dream about. He decides to invest his wealth and resources in a hedonistic lifestyle of pleasure and productivity. Dive in, and – deny, deny, deny. So begins his exploration of the human heart.

Solomon becomes a party animal. He drinks the wine. He embraces the festivities with mindless mirth and laughter. Then he begins his many building projects and padding his own nest. His palace was opulent and grand. He surrounded it with vast gardens and water features. He had more than enough servants to maintain them and to rigorously assist him as an individual.[6]

'Heh, Uri, peel me a grape.'

'Right on, your highness.'

Then he goes on shopping sprees and hoards it all. He collects gold and silver coins and surrounds himself with priceless objets d'art.[7] He also rustles up livestock and horses for his ranch.[8] He soon surpasses every other would-be cowboy before him. Texans would stand in awe. Yet it doesn't stop here. He also acquires the best music on the market and commissions live concerts at the palace.[9]

Solomon was living the life of a rock star, but what's a rock star without their groupies? So he starts his own harem, which eventually morphs into a religious menagerie. Seven hundred wives and three hundred concubines surround him in the royal court.[10] One thousand more reasons to deny, deny, deny.

Money, sex, and power – no half measures here. Solomon had all the resources, and he exploited them to the max in his search for the meaning of life. Do you want to know what he learned during those years of indulgence? It may surprise you.

> I denied myself nothing my eyes desired;
>   I refused my heart no pleasure.
> My heart took delight in all my labour,
>   and this was the reward for all my toil.
> Yet when I surveyed all that my hands had done
>   and what I had toiled to achieve,
> everything was meaningless, a chasing after the wind;
>   nothing was gained under the sun.
>
> *(Eccl. 2:10–11)*

It's kind of sad where his wisdom led him, isn't it? The remainder of Ecclesiastes expands on these first two chapters as Solomon further reflects on all he has observed and witnessed throughout his meaningless life.

So should we take his word for it? He was the wisest man on the planet. Is it really all meaningless? How can we be awesome if everything we put our hands to is trifling and inconsequential? Is this a gateway to the dark side? Where is the wisdom in this puzzling book?

It's here, but you have to pay attention. The wisdom is found in one word that pops up thirty-two times throughout this grand experiment, and that word is 'under' – under the sun and under heaven. This says it all. The spatial boundaries of Solomon's test were limited to space, time and this physical world. What he is saying in his inscrutable way is that all life on this planet without a God-connection is utterly meaningless – a complete waste of time.[11] But why is that?

Aren't we created to flourish in this world? This is our God-given place in the universe. We are dust, and to dust we shall return. We are physical. We are carbon-based units made to thrive and live in this world under the sun, so why aren't we content with the current situation? The animal kingdom isn't bothered by some spiritual deity. Why do we have the compulsion to drag God, or a god, into our lives?

Divine Microchip

I often tell people that one of the most profound truths of the Old Testament is the poem summarizing Solomon's musings. It encapsulates his reflections on the human drama. You are probably familiar with it. Surprisingly, it was put to music and eventually became a hit song. It was recorded in 1965 by the Byrds. The song was 'Turn, Turn, Turn'.[1] It was classic rock at some of its best. When I first heard it as a teenager, I had no idea I was listening to 'classic Bible' at some of its best.

> There is a time for everything,
>> and a season for every activity *under the heavens*:
> a time to be born and a time to die,
>> a time to plant and a time to uproot,
> a time to kill and a time to heal,
>> a time to tear down and a time to build,
> a time to weep and a time to laugh,
>> a time to mourn and a time to dance,
> a time to scatter stones and a time to gather them,
>> a time to embrace and a time to refrain from embracing,
> a time to search and a time to give up,
>> a time to keep and a time to throw away,
> a time to tear and a time to mend,
>> a time to be silent and a time to speak,
> a time to love and a time to hate,
>> a time for war and a time for peace.
>
> *(Eccl. 3:1–8, italics mine)*

Notice in line two – there's that phrase again: 'under the heavens'. On this planet, we are bound by space and time, and nothing endures. Everything has a beginning and an end. Nothing lasts forever. The cycle continues to go round and round. The wisdom of this poem is that a season is just that – a season. Don't despair when things are bad, because this too will pass. We go from one season to another – a time to be born and a time to die; a time to weep and a time to laugh. This is now the natural order of things in the physical world of space and time. It's the cycle we were born into. It's all we know, so why the discontent?

What's the problem? The problem is God himself. Solomon exposes us to a conspiracy theory that reaches all the way to the top. God made us for space and time, but he has also implanted us with a divine microchip that compels us to look up and say, 'There must be more than this.'

> He has made everything beautiful in its *time*. He has also set *eternity* in the human heart; yet no one can fathom what God has done from beginning to end.
>
> *(Eccl. 3:11, italics mine)*

God has lodged a spiritual tracker at the very core of our existence, and it won't stop beeping until we fall into his arms. Solomon calls that tracker 'eternity'. God has embedded eternity in the human heart. Of course, this isn't an earthly microchip but a spiritual longing, an inner ache that compels us to reach beyond what is known, hoping to find completeness. The fact that we were created in the image of God enhances this yearning and hunger. When there is a disconnect between the imagers and the Image-giver, the tracer goes off until we are reunited or we refuse to answer.

If the Almighty had left us alone without the implant, we would be content with our lot. Solomon would have discovered meaning and purpose under the sun, but knowing there is more than meets the eye on our planet brings its own discontent.

If we feel we are missing out on something, we are not satisfied until we find it, experience it and participate in it. This is the way we were made to be. It's probably why we ate from the wrong tree in the garden of Eden. We just couldn't stop ourselves. Knowing there is more than space and time; knowing there is this other realm, this other dimension; this other Being who hides himself in eternity and wants to be found by each of us, makes life in this world meaningless without him.

Solomon was seeking the *joie de vivre* – the joy of living. It was lost on him in his daily search and multiple activities under the sun. He despaired at the mundane. He was looking for inspiration and enlightenment, something beyond himself and his existence on this earth.

We hear the beeping of the divine tracker because we were created in the image of God. The other creatures of the earth can't hear it. Eternity isn't calling to them because they don't bear that image and they don't have the implant. They aren't longing for more or looking up, wondering what lurks beyond the ozone. They are quite content with the natural order of things; we aren't. Although we as humans get it wrong and go down many, many paths in our attempts to encounter what lies beyond our natural existence, we can't help but shout into the sky and howl, 'There must be more than this!'

The divine tracker compels us to look up and answer the call buried in the pages of Ecclesiastes. Many try to ignore, deny, and quash it, but it's hard work trying to suppress the implant with our natural mind and intellect as it writhes, thrashes, and fights for attention in the human heart.

> You, God, are my God,
>> earnestly I seek you;
> I thirst for you,
>> my whole being longs for you,
> in a dry and parched land
>> where there is no water.

(Ps. 63:1)

Some of you may be thinking that a tracker is something a spy clips under cars, slips into purses, or drops into pockets to track our movements. Predictably, trackers are embedded in our phones, laptops and tablets. This is not a conspiracy theory; this is what the 'location services' on our phones and devices are doing each time we switch them on.

However, God's eternity-microchip-tracker doesn't work this way. He already knows where we are. He implanted the tracker so that we would know *where he is* – his location. It awakens us to his presence, his reality, and when he is moving or doing something special around us. The chip is for our benefit, not his. It alerts us when he is near. It signals us when he is speaking. Evidently, God wants us to find him and grow more sensitive to his presence.[2]

> Seek the LORD while he may be found;
>> call on him while he is near.

(Isa. 55:6)

> My heart has heard you say, 'Come and talk with me.'
>   And my heart responds, 'LORD, I am coming.'
>
> *(Ps. 27:8, NLT)*

This is the wisdom of Ecclesiastes, as depicted in the musings of Solomon. This is the challenge: don't fight who you are. Don't ignore the summons to reach out.

> You will seek me and find me when you seek me with all your heart.
>
> *(Jer. 29:13)*

The angst of Ecclesiastes is no longer our story because Jesus has bridged the disconnect between the imager and the Image-giver.[3] He has spanned the gap between time, space and eternity – life on earth and the heavenly realm. However, when we drift and embrace this world more than the values of eternity, the beeper in our heart goes off like a fire alarm. We have to drink the nectar of heaven or die. If we try to suppress or attempt to switch the beeper off, we will lose the supernatural edge God gave us to navigate this world.

> Now all has been heard;
>   here is the conclusion of the matter:
> fear God and keep his commandments,
>   for this is the duty of all mankind.
>
> *(Eccl. 12:13)*

20. Face in the Mirror

What is our place in the vast matrix we call creation? The great majority doesn't know. You can hear the divine microchip going off all through our towns and cities.

- Who am I?
- What am I?
- Where do I fit in?
- There must be more than this.

For many, the boat drifts without an anchor. We have unmoored ourselves from the truth of heaven, and we don't know what shore we should steer towards. Philosophers, governments, scientists, the media, and even our entertainment industry try to silence the beeper going off in our hearts. This will never satisfy us.

What does it mean to be human? We can't be awesome in this world if we don't know who we are and the God who created us. The fact that we are fashioned in the image of God is more than a religious fairy tale, but what does it mean? A divine revelation of who we are is what triggers our faith to clothe ourselves with Christ. It's what inspires us. The potential is there; we just need to align our hearts and minds with God's revelation.

God created a zoo. The animals flourished. Everything was accessible: the sanctuary, food, and water. There was ample supply. The creatures had freedom to roam and settle in the fields, sky, lakes, meadows, and forests – all provided by the Creator. It was a wonderful safari park. The Bible calls it Eden.

To assume control of the park, God invested himself in Adam and Eve. He created us in his image. The Almighty wants more than a game reserve; he wants friends – friends who think like him, friends who value what he values,[1] someone relatable, someone who can accept and handle responsibility. We reflect his glory.

This is what defines us and sets us apart from all the other creatures roaming the planet. Without the image of God stamped on us, we're just part of the zoo. When you get rid of the imager and deny we were created in God's likeness, life becomes cheap and disposable.[2] Ignore it, and we lose our way, our destiny, our purpose, and our focus. We no longer know who or what we are. It's an identity crisis.

Evolutionists may reject the divine and attach an ape or Neanderthal to our family tree, but they can't ignore the fact that we are unique and we are spiritually drawn to our Creator – it appears we also want a friend. This is evident no matter what narrative we embrace regarding primordial events and processes. The divine microchip just keeps on beeping.

In the revolt, we fell short of the glory. We were stripped as naked as the animals. The glory was gone, and we've been struggling to restore it ever since. So we spend our lives sewing together fig leaves.[3] We fascinate ourselves with celebrities, models, designer clothes, status sports cars, wonderful stuff, power and money, reflections in the mirror, cosmetic surgery, and uncountable selfies. We have grown so accustomed to the practice that we forget how awesome the Creator God actually is and what it means to bear his likeness. Whose face are we looking at when we stand in front of the mirror? Are we concerned about his image or ours?

The fact that we are created in the image of God is a big deal. It's easy to take it for granted, but it's how God made us and how heaven defines us. We were created to be like God – perfect like God, holy like God, reborn into the image of Christ, who is God. Our DNA is stamped with greatness. We have this gene buried in our genetic make-up. We haven't left it behind in Eden; we have just lost the capacity to fully embrace it and let it shine. It's hard to be awesome or even motivated towards the sublime if we keep looking into a dirty, cracked and broken mirror and do not accept and grow into the image God has set before us. If we are no longer awed by God then we have looked at our own image far too long.

When the revelation of the image of God was first publicized through the book of Genesis, scholarly tongues began to wag. Today we have a vast historical library of books, articles, letters, sermons and descriptions, about what this image thingy actually is. Biblically, our identity is bound to it.

Spanning the many centuries of study and intellectual discussion, I think we are all ready to hear the conclusion of the matter, aren't we? What exactly is the image of God that we bear? We are interested because it's about us. It describes who we are. It distinguishes our role and place in this vast universe. So what is the scholarly consensus regarding the image of God? Heaven knows theologians throughout the generations have had long enough to discuss it. Do you want to know their conclusion? Well, brace yourself – there isn't one. It doesn't exist. You will not find a scholarly consensus or a unified definition of the image of God.

There are many ideas,[4] but no one has yet provided a compelling argument or description that is satisfactory. In search of the elusive definition, we compare ourselves to the animal kingdom and point out the differences, thinking that's where we will find the answer. Unlike animals, we communicate with a sophisticated language and a vast vocabulary; we have abstract thought; we are extremely creative; and we're fuelled by reason, not instinct. Some say this points to the image of God stamped on humanity.

I won't argue with this conclusion, but the comparison method seems a bit one-sided and arbitrary. What about the superior attributes of other living creatures? Some could beat us at arm-wrestling. We lack clarity with regard to our place and purpose in the universe, while animals seem content just to get on with it. As for longevity, we sure don't last long – our sell-by date comes quicker than any of us desire. Elephants are larger than we are. Apes are stronger. Sharks live longer. Porpoises might be smarter; killer whales and chimpanzees are self-aware like us; scientists say cockroaches will outlive us after a nuclear holocaust. If not for the image of God, I doubt we would've survived in this world, and we certainly wouldn't have been at the top of the food chain. The point is that this method seems a bit thin on the ground when we talk about the image of God.

Then we come to the popular notion that the image is all about ethics. We are accountable, moral beings.[5] We understand what our parents, human and divine, mean when they say, 'Behave yourself.' When we are caught doing something wrong, we normally wrestle with guilt and shame. We experience relief and hope when pardoned or forgiven. This, scholars have argued, is a major component regarding the image of God.

Another school of thought concentrates on our divine remit as planet caretakers.[6] We are to watch over this world and care for the animals in it. We are stamped with God's image to rule. We represent him to lesser creatures. We are the cardholders of heaven; the task force drafted from above. We are the divinely appointed governors of earth. This view is widely endorsed; but when we step outside the boundaries of Genesis, to say we can walk on two legs, hold a conversation, and do a bit of gardening is a bit of a cop-out.

Others consider our physicality.[7] They say we look like God even though he's described as an invisible spirit.[8] Nonetheless, the Bible doesn't flinch when it speaks of God revealing himself in a spiritual body.[9] It's difficult getting our heads around this one; maybe we need to stretch our theology.[10] There is some semantic mileage to this definition,[11] but there are just as many theological stances refuting it.[12]

Perhaps we get hung up on this because we're concentrating on God the Father and bypassing the Trinity. God the Son has a body. When he ascended into heaven, he was in a human frame.[13] When he returns, he will still be in his divine human form. When Jesus took on human flesh and likeness, it wasn't for a limited period of time. He will always be fully human and fully divine. I don't want to go down a rabbit hole here, but theologically, humanity is created in the image of God, not the other way around. Also, the fact that Jesus is still fully human and fully God ruling from heaven suggests that the image of God in humanity is more than just a few attributes or responsibilities to care for the planet. Perhaps our chronology and time-based, linear way of thinking cloud the issue.

Jesus often defined himself as the Son of Man.[14] However, he wasn't referring to the weak, naked position of defrocked, fallen flesh. He came to reveal what the image of God stamped on humanity was supposed to look like. It was glorious.

The New Testament is clear on this issue. 'The Son is the radiance of God's glory and the exact representation of his being.'[15] The Son is the image of the invisible God.[16] Christ is the glory of God's image.[17] God intends to conform us into the image of his Son.[18]

Over time, there has been a tendency to compartmentalize and reduce the image to manageable sound bites. We compare ourselves to other creatures and draw distinctions. We categorize and isolate various qualities and hold them up as God's image. This method is logical but quite selective. The results have been limited and unsatisfactory. I believe one drawback is that we tend to focus on the image-bearer more than the greatness of the Image-giver.[19] If we had seen Adam and Eve before they were stripped and unclothed and had lost their glory, we wouldn't have been asking so many questions. Jesus, the second Adam, arrives and shows us what that former glory looked like.

Our bodies, or glorified bodies, will follow us throughout eternity, just as the body of Jesus will clothe him through all the ages. Is it theologically anathema to say the image needs no interpretation but should be accepted at face value: body, soul, mind, and spirit?[20] Does it need further definition? Jesus has shown us what it is, what it looks like and how it behaves. If Jesus had disposed of his human body, he would have discarded his humanity. If we end up as unclothed spirits, we too would no longer be fully human, created in the image of God.[21]

For we know that when this earthly tent we live in is taken down (that is, when we die and leave this earthly body), we will have a house in heaven, an *eternal body* made for us by God himself and not by human hands. We grow weary in our present bodies, and we long to put on our heavenly bodies like new clothing. For we will put on heavenly bodies; we will not be spirits without bodies. While we live in these earthly bodies, we groan and sigh, but it's not that we want to die and get rid of these bodies that clothe us. Rather, we want to put on our new bodies so that these dying bodies will be swallowed up by life. God himself has prepared us for this, *and as a guarantee he has given us his Holy Spirit.*

(2 Cor. 5:1–5, NLT, italics mine)[22]

Today, I come to God as a child. I hold up the image. It's battered, bruised, broken and fractured, like a toy I damaged through carelessness and neglect. I hold it up to my father in tears.

'Daddy, I broke it. Can you fix it?'

'I can. I will, I am.'

'What will it look like?'

'It will look like my much-loved son, Jesus Christ, in whom I am well pleased.'

Consider the glory displayed at the transfiguration.[1] Watch the way Jesus handles his body. The way he walks in nature,[2] how he deals with people,[3] and in the face of opposition.[4] Listen to his words. His motivation is love.[5] He does nothing and says nothing until he gets the go-ahead from his Father.[6] He is the perfect representation of the Almighty. If we keep looking to him, we will become like him. We will become whole and complete, moving from glory to glory.

> Now the Lord is the Spirit, and where the Spirit of the Lord is, there is freedom. And we all, who with unveiled faces contemplate the Lord's glory, *are being transformed into his image with ever-increasing glory*, which comes from the Lord, *who is the Spirit*.
>
> *(2 Cor. 3:17–18, italics mine)*

Can you grasp what is being said here? Paul is saying, don't look anywhere else in trying to figure out what the image of

God is in humanity. Look at God himself. Then our eyes will be opened. Then we will understand who we are and how great the restoration actually is that's taking place in us at this very moment. The goal is the glory of God in the face of humanity. God never instructed us to source the image through creature comparisons or compartmentalized attributes. We discover who we are in relation to the Creator, not the creation.

In the beginning, God didn't rest until his creation was perfect.[7] He won't rest again until excellence and glory are restored. Do you really think you were born without purpose or direction? Do you actually presume the image of God is just an added feature to enable zookeepers? We were created to reflect God's brilliance in love, spirit, physicality, character and mental acuteness. It's not locked away for some future event, but it's being restored and activated right now. God is doing everything to re-establish the glory that we so gullibly surrendered.

The god of this world forfeited the world above.[8] Sin is always a downward movement. The evil forces are always descending: from heaven to earth,[9] from earth to the pit,[10] into hell,[11] and then the lake of fire.[12] The crime of Eden has made us more a creature of this earth than of heaven. The balance is wrong. God is always trying to get us to look up and not be so fixated on this fallen planet and the principalities and powers that steer it.[13] This is one of the reasons God calls us to worship him. We need to focus on and value him and what's above.[14]

Sin drags us down, not up. The fall isn't just a one-off event; it is also an ongoing process. The world isn't fallen; it's falling. God continually steps in to decelerate the process. If we don't keep our eyes fixed on Jesus and continually look up, then we will descend with the world. The downward pull is relentless and constant.[15]

> Since, then, you have been raised with Christ, set your hearts on things above, where Christ is, seated at the right hand of God. Set your minds on things above, not on earthly things. For you died, and your life is now hidden with Christ in God. When Christ, who is your life, appears, then *you also will appear with him in glory.*
>
> *(Col. 3:1–4, italics mine)*[16]

The world is off balance, and the faster it descends, the more biased it becomes. We tear down all the God-given boundaries that promote life and wellbeing. We call evil good and good evil.[17] God kicked Adam and Eve out of the garden, so we returned the favour and kicked him out of our lives. We put him off and stand naked in a hostile world, thinking we can navigate it on our own. Then we blame God for all the chaos and mayhem. A spirit of deception can influence an entire nation, generation and people group. The spiritual world abhors a vacuum, and the forces of this world will take advantage of any empty space we leave open to them.

The means God uses to slow down this gradual descent into chaos is the Holy Spirit in the hearts of all true believers who follow Jesus Christ.[18] Every act of love and compassion holds back hate. Every act of forgiveness holds back the world's thirst for revenge. Every 'no' that is said in the face of temptation is a 'yes' to the life of God on this planet. Every prayer and act of worship to the Creator ushers in his earthly kingdom. Every faithful martyr declares the glory of heaven and the worthiness of Christ.

Of course, many do good deeds throughout the world because the image of God will leak out somewhere, but the glory of that image is only found in Jesus Christ. We all have sinned; however, Paul didn't say we fell short of sinlessness; he said we fell short of the glory of God.[19] This is what we fail to live up to. This is what Adam and Eve recognized after they ate from the tree. They were naked. The glory was gone. The image was clouded. The restored image is the glory of God. The glory of God and the glory reflected in the image are the same.[20] God is restoring the divine image in the face of Jesus Christ, God himself – God the Son.[21]

The image of God is not something we have; it's who we are. To deny it is to deny ourselves; it is a disavowal of reality. When we behave like animals, the glory of the image dims to an undefined shadow. The glory of the image is quenched when we elevate this world over the next. The glory of the image can be stifled, and that comes with a heavy price. The truth is, we will never be fulfilled in this life until we accept and live up to who we are.

There is a tendency to curse ourselves when we sin. We loathe ourselves as people. We beat ourselves up, hoping to procure some resolution or favour with God as we confess and repent of our sin. This is not biblical or conducive to our mental and spiritual health. We are often quick to quote, 'Hate the sin but love the sinner', but have a difficult time applying this principle to ourselves.

To hate yourself as a person created in the image of God is not honouring to the Creator or pleasing to the God who called you. This is not the position we should take or revel in when we sin. It's misdirected angst. It opens us up to despair and dejection. The spiritual forces of harm love it when we reject ourselves as children of God born from above and cleansed through the blood of Jesus Christ.

My war is not with myself as a person; my battle is with the sin that sometimes overtakes me. I am still a child of God. I am still called to be like his Son. I am still created in his image. I am not rejected. I am still the prodigal son who the Father sees coming up the road and runs out to reinstate and clothe. I am not the anomaly that blights creation – sin is the anomaly.[22] My repugnance and anger should be directed at sin, not towards myself as a child of God. Self-hatred is not heaven's solution for wrongdoing. Consider Judas and where a revulsion of self led him.

I am a child of the living God, created in the image of God. I am his creation. I am seated with Christ in heavenly places. I have the mind of Christ.[23] I carry the treasure of the Holy Spirit in my mortal body. I am being transformed right now into his image and glory. Hopefully, every day when I look in the mirror of my life, I will see more of him and less of my selfishness. This is the reality I choose to live in, and this is the faith and narrow path I will follow: by his grace, in his love and through his sacrifice. We have not seen him, but we love him because he first loved us.[24]

Many yearn for the second coming of Jesus Christ in our generation, but we should also long for his tangible presence in our lives right now. I am not sitting back, waiting for Jesus to reboot the planet; he's already started the process – Christ in me, not in the clouds. I want to know Christ today; in every encounter, in every transaction, in each decision, in every book I read, on each page of his Bible, and in every conversation I choose to enter. If I knew Jesus was coming tomorrow, there is nothing I would change in my life today. He would not be a stranger, and eternity would not be an odd or foreign place to be because, in my heart, I already live there with him.

Many of us have the habit of listening or reading but not adopting. Children seem to assume lifestyles and world-views much easier than we adults do. When I was around 10 years old, I went to the cinema and watched *The Day of the Triffids* – all by myself. This was before movie ratings (I saw a lot of things I shouldn't have while growing up). At the time, I wished I hadn't seen that one. It scared me half to death. It left such an impression on me that I was afraid to walk home when I left the cinema. I was constantly looking over my shoulder. I stuck close to the porches I passed in case I had to make a run for it. I just didn't want to be eaten by a plant that had a taste for human flesh. Those triffids were nasty creatures. In my little head they were lurking behind every tree and bush I had to pass. What's embarrassing is that the sun was shining and it wasn't even dark out. Now, I wasn't a wimp, but I sure was impressionable. I didn't just watch the movie screen; I had adopted the world-view of that creepy universe. The narrative of the story quickly became my new reality, and it followed me all the way home: shudder.

I don't believe I was odd as a child, but I had a hard time shaking off the world-view of specific stories. Perhaps this is why so many children are afraid of monsters lurking under their beds. They not only hear a story; they also adopt the world-view it's couched in. As adults, we've trained ourselves not to do this.

We have all developed sophisticated, fine-tuned filters to guard the reality we choose to embrace. Some people filter out the existence of flying saucers and extraterrestrial encounters. Others take it quite seriously. They invite them into their cosmology and join SETI, hoping to make contact.[1] The fringe group wrap aluminium foil on top of their heads and duck around corners when they see a shape-shifter. Crop circles are secret messages from the greys – you know, those little aliens with the big bulgy eyes incarcerated in Area 51.

We all, to some extent, adopt the world we want to live in: flat earth, hollow earth, angels, incantations, ghosts, extraterrestrials, demons, vampires, zombies, miracles, microchips in vaccinations, along with the never-ending sludge of conspiracy theories. I'm sure your filter was turned on just by reading this list. Some ideas we outright reject, others we question, and still others we assume or are tempted to embrace.

What we need to be aware of is that the filter of our reality gauge is also fine-tuned and active when we pick up our Bibles and step into the world-view of the ancient Near East. At times we struggle because the biblical world-view is so foreign to our present lifestyle and because the standard is supernaturally high.

Have you been adjusting your reality gauge as you read this book? I wonder, what you have filtered out so far? Perhaps you have replaced the word 'awesome' with a tamer, more down-to-earth word or concept? Is the call to be like God unfeasible? Is the challenge to be Jesus in this world a super-spiritual notion – a religious hyperbole not to be taken seriously? What about holiness, or being as holy as God is holy? That, too, can seem a daunting obstacle.

What we need to hold onto, though, is that we are God's project.[2] He is the potter.[3] Our faith is in him, not in ourselves.

Keep looking up and consider the greatness of God, not the weaknesses and limitations that often sneak up and bite us. It has nothing to do with the mask collection in our closet. Primarily, we're learning how to let go and not hold the knowledge of good and evil so tightly. This is difficult in faith and in practice, but it's certainly not impossible. God is our perfection. Coming to terms with this is the reality we have to accept if we want to step out of the boat, take the risk, and embrace the adventure set before us.

23. Be Christ in the Room

I once attended a two-day prayer conference in Scotland. I was sitting in a crowd of superheroes. A faithful group of pastors arrived to intercede and seek God for their communities and for each other. These people had fought the battles, bore the brunt and faithfully preached the Scriptures. Some of them were hurting; some wore the scars. It was an honour to be among them. We were all growing into the robes handed to us. The image was being restored as we looked to Jesus and to each other. I can't help but revere and salute these warriors of love. They are a holy gift to the church.

During one of the silent prayer sessions, my attention was drawn to a middle-aged pastor sitting across from me. The room was quiet, and everyone had their eyes closed. As I watched him, I could hear God say, 'That is a man of prayer. I hear his prayers, and I am going to send him workers.' That was it.

Like most people would, I wondered if this was really God or not. The message was so general and simple. I thought this could apply to any pastor in any church, but I am learning that, if you want to be awesome and adventurous, you have to step out and do some crazy things. So I walked over to him, knelt down, and whispered, 'I believe God just told me you are a man of prayer, that he hears your prayers, and he is going to send you workers.'

I wasn't sure he heard me at first because he didn't move, but seconds later he looked up and said, 'You have no idea what you just did.' Then he closed his eyes and continued to pray as though I wasn't there.

Sometimes you get it right; sometimes you don't. However, the next day was enlightening. He came over to me and said:

> Richard, I just want to tell you what happened yesterday. As I was sitting there praying, I was confronting God. I told him I didn't think he was listening to me or answering any of my prayers. I am doing everything by myself, and I am exhausted. I keep asking him to send me helpers, but they don't come. I was praying, 'Lord, I am weary. I'm going to turn in my credentials and leave if I don't hear from you today. Here I am; if you have something to say, please tell me now because I really need to hear it.' Richard, that's when you came over and spoke those words to me.

I was humbled and astounded. God is so good to those who love him. He cares, and he meets us right where we are. Put on Christ. Be like Jesus in the world. That day, if no one had listened and obeyed, this never would have happened. The church would have lost another wounded soldier because we were afraid to walk across the room and follow in the footsteps of the Messiah.

Consider the encounter Jesus had with the woman at the well.[1] That brief, Holy Spirit-led conversation triggered a messianic revival in her nearby village. The Father lives his life through his Son,[2] as we let Jesus live his life through us. It all transpires in, by and through the Holy Spirit, who is God.[3]

The more we set our minds on the things above and expect Jesus to live his life through us, the more opportunities we have to display that image to the world. It's another surge of faith and growth in the God-given robes that clothe us.

The adventure-driven life is not just for our neighbour, our pastor, or those we deem more special or holy than ourselves; it's to be the lifestyle of every believer who follows Jesus Christ. It's not hidden in the sweet bye and bye but is evidenced in the violent, scary, chaotic, irrational, messy and confusing here and now. God is working in and through all of us. By faith, put on Christ. Paul wasn't playing some false humility gig when he told us:

> God chose the foolish things of the world to shame the wise; God chose the weak things of the world to shame the strong. God chose the lowly things of this world and the despised things – and the things that are not – to nullify the things that are, so that no one may boast before him. *It is because of him* that you are in Christ Jesus, who has become for us wisdom from God – that is, our righteousness, holiness and redemption.
>
> *(1 Cor. 1:27–30, italics mine)*

I used to look out and feel so disconnected and small. Solomon was right: life under the sun is meaningless if I don't connect with the One who dwells beyond the created universe. A few years ago, during one of those uncomfortable moments when I was philosophically flailing about in a pool of emotional insignificance, I heard the voice of God speak in my heart. 'If I, the Creator of heaven and earth, live inside of you, you are not small, and you are definitely not insignificant.' This revelation floored me. How can I ever entertain deceptive thoughts of disconnection and triviality again?

It is an honour to bear the image of God, but to become a host of the Almighty at the very core of our being is beyond comprehension. We carry this treasure in our earthly bodies.[4]

This is all part of the history. It began with God and will end with God – the Alpha and the Omega.[5] God creates us in his image. Then he plants eternity in our hearts. We respond to that divine impulse. He clothes us with Jesus. We are in the process of growing and maturing. We are becoming more like him. The image is being restored but, instead of working from the outside in, as with Adam, God is now working from the inside out.

We are the temple of the living God.[6] The image of God isn't just a few isolated characteristics we lord over the animals or have in common with the heavenly host. We are the image, but the cross takes it to another level. The image is now much more than a reflection from above; it is also a living, active, speaking presence from within. Christ in you and Christ in us is the hope of glory.[7] This is the matrix of awe and wonder! The world and our community need to see who Jesus is and what he is like. With bold faith, we let him shine – the glory will be his, the adventure will be ours!

PART FOUR

The Identity

As a film, I really like *Braveheart*. There's a nobility to it, and it inspires me. It's a semi-historical account of Sir William Wallace. In the thirteenth century, he led the fight for Scottish independence. I had the privilege of viewing his sword during a family holiday.[1] It is big and heavy and requires two hands to swing it. The Scots call it, 'Freedom's Sword'.

The most rousing scene of the movie is when Wallace is captured and laid spread-eaglewise on a wooden cross. His torturer keeps asking him to recant his rebellion as the Scottish citizens watch on in horror. The crowd can hardly endure it, so they start shouting for Wallace to surrender and put an end to the ordeal. The drama is intense. Then comes the pause, a brief moment of silence as Wallace lifts his head and defiantly shouts, 'Freeeeedom!'

Sometimes we don't fully appreciate the liberty God extends to us. The loudest cry for freedom on this planet came from the cross of Jesus Christ: 'Father, forgive them.' That shout still echoes through the ages. We can never forget it.[2]

It is for freedom that Christ has set us free. Stand firm, then, and do not let yourselves be burdened again by a yoke of slavery.

(Gal. 5:1)

The Spirit who gives life has set you free from the law of sin and death.

(Rom. 8:2)

Now the Lord is the Spirit, and where the Spirit of the Lord is, there is freedom.

(2 Cor. 3:17)

So if the Son sets you free, you will be free indeed.

(John 8:36)

Our umbilical cord to this earth is uncut, and we cannot break it, or wrestle free. It's the source of all we know and the sphere from which we draw every breath. God the Father picked up the cross, and he swung it. It was heaven's sword of freedom. His aim was determined and perfect. It hit its target and sliced through the umbilical cord that was tying us to this world and the things in it. We have been reborn into a kingdom not made, designed or established by human hands or based upon worldly wisdom. It is not governed by people. It's governed by the One who sits beyond everything we know, the One who stepped into our playground for thirty-three years but was never tainted by it.

This world, its behaviour, influence, attractions and failures have no grip on him. He arrived on this planet from the outside: a divine seed from beyond, miraculously imbedded in a human womb. Jesus is the Divine Other, the Outsider, the Invader, the Deliverer who came from the realm of love: the kingdom of God.[3] As Jesus said, 'I am not of this world.'[4]

When God cut our umbilical cord to this planet, we died, and no Christian survived the operation. This is the wisdom of God. We have been deleted from the worldly programme – erased. Our old self is not saved somewhere in the cosmic computer to be retrieved at a later date. Our old self is not in heaven being polished, fixed or repaired. The old self is gone, lost, kaput, forgotten, silenced – dead. This is how God saves us from ourselves – we have been executed.[5]

This is why, in faith, we have to take off the old self – it's a cadaver. Igor may tempt us to dig up our sinful past and beat ourselves over the head with it; but it's still the miscreant God has deleted. We are no longer the caricature of Frankenstein's monster. We are born again; all things have become new – transformed and being transformed.[6] We no longer have to listen to the voices of this world. We listen to the voice that speaks to us from beyond.[7] The unassimilated Other has severed our umbilical cord to this planet. If we are going to embark on this awesome adventure with God, we must accept this one truth: I am no longer of this world.[8] Yee-haw!

Where do we fit in since we are no longer cardholders of this planet? The world often tries to define us. The Jews called us Nazarenes.[1] The citizens of Antioch were the first to call us Christians.[2] What criteria does the world employ as it seeks to define, accept or reject us? Do they watch what we do? Do they scrutinize our character, goals and behaviour? Do they evaluate our conversation? Do our words stretch empirical truth? Are we devoted to the life we proclaim? Is our love noteworthy and authentic? Are we like Jesus Christ?[3] These are some of the benchmarks the world applies as it probes our assertions. These questions are logical because they stem from the wisdom of the world.[4]

Here's one assessment I find disturbing, yet challenging: 'I like your Christ; I do not like your Christians. Your Christians are so unlike your Christ,' said Mahatma Gandhi. Ouch! Is this an accurate evaluation? Looking from the outside, I think we have all questioned the behaviour of some who confess the name. However, these words focus on the robe we claim to wear but ignore the fact that we are in a process of growth to fill that garment. The world would like to see Christ's fullness and character exhibited through us, but so would we. We can't let the pace of our progress discourage us. Love never fails.[5] As Paul says, 'Who are you to judge someone else's servant? To their own master, servants stand or fall. And they will stand, for the Lord is able to make them stand.'[6] We are no longer of this world, so how can the world accurately define us? It can't.[7]

The wind blows wherever it pleases. You hear its sound, but you cannot tell where it comes from or where it is going. So it is with everyone born of the Spirit.

(John 3:8)

Biblically speaking, there is only one characteristic that separates the Christian from the world and the people living in it – do you host the Holy Spirit? Is the Holy Spirit alive in you? That is the assessment: this is the bottom line that defines a Christian. The caveat is that we cannot receive the Holy Spirit outside of Jesus Christ.[8] It was his sacrifice for our sin on the cross that made us holy and righteous enough to receive the eternal, indwelling of his Spirit. God moved from the holy of holies to the heart of every believer who repents and embraces the gospel.[9]

The Bible is full of illustrations describing the character and life of a Christian in this world. We are salt.[10] We are light.[11] We are athletes running a race.[12] We are pilgrims heading towards a divinely ordered destination,[13] but I'm particularly attracted to the way the Apostle Paul describes himself. It's worth exploring because if anyone lived an awesome, adventurous life, it was the Apostle Paul.

Therefore, if anyone is in Christ, the new creation has come: the old has gone, the new is here! . . . *We are therefore Christ's ambassadors*, as though God were making his appeal through us.

(2 Cor. 5:17–20, italics mine)

Pray also for me, that whenever I speak, words may be given me so that I will fearlessly make known the mystery of the gospel, for which *I am an ambassador* in chains.

(Eph. 6:19–20, italics mine)

Paul calls himself an ambassador. Have you ever defined, or thought of yourself as an ambassador of Christ, or an ambassador of the kingdom of God? Is this a path that leads to awesomeness? It's the one the Apostle Paul travelled. The fact that he wrote more than a quarter of the New Testament from this position is quite remarkable.

So how do we define ourselves as Christians? Do we look in the mirror and see an athletic pilgrim of salt and light in the middle of a race staring back at us? It's a rather humorous and nebulous way to describe ourselves, and it certainly needs a lot of unpacking. For the pragmatist, these terms are abstract and allegorical. Contrast this to the word 'ambassador' and we enter the sphere of social science, political agendas and international relationships. To identify ourselves as ambassadors of Jesus Christ and the kingdom of God may get us killed[14] but not misunderstood. It's a loaded perspective.

Our passports to this world have been revoked, but we are not abandoned citizens. God has issued each of us a new passport. It's red. It's embossed with a cross. The country of our allegiance is stamped on the cover. It reads, 'The kingdom of God'. We are not of this world, but neither is the country we represent.[1]

Paul was a Hebrew Pharisee holding a passport to Rome.[2] On this planet, he had respect, power and influence. He was assimilated like everyone else born into the system, but the moment he pledged his allegiance to the King of heaven and received his kingdom credentials, he was no longer a part of this world. He re-examined his life and the plague of sin from God's perspective. The shadow was lifted from his eyes and heart. He realized his religious zeal was misdirected – an affront to God. His worldly credentials were anti-Christ. His life was an assault against heaven.

Jesus grabbed hold of Paul and violently overturned the tables in his heart. His transition from Pharisee to God's ambassador was traumatic.[3] Just like his ancestor Solomon, Paul re-evaluated the meaning of life under the sun and found it wanting. It was empty and vain. 'Meaningless! Meaningless! Utterly meaningless! Everything is meaningless.'[4]

. . . even though we can list what many might think are impressive credentials. You know my pedigree: a legitimate birth, circumcised on the eighth day; an Israelite from the elite tribe of Benjamin; a strict and devout adherent to God's law; a fiery defender of the purity of my religion, even to the point of persecuting Christians; a meticulous observer of everything set down in God's law Book.

The very credentials these people are waving around as something special, I'm tearing up and throwing out with the trash – along with everything else I used to take credit for. And why? Because of Christ. *Yes, all the things I once thought were so important are gone from my life. Compared to the high privilege of knowing Christ Jesus as my Master, firsthand, everything I once thought I had going for me is insignificant – dog dung. I've dumped it all in the trash so that I could embrace Christ and be embraced by him.* I didn't want some petty, inferior brand of righteousness that comes from keeping a list of rules when I could get the robust kind that comes from trusting Christ – *God's* righteousness.

(Phil. 3:4–9, MSG, italics mine, except in final sentence)

Paul's conversion required training like that of the other disciples before him.[5] He had put on Christ, now he had to grow into what was accredited him – not for salvation but for the kingdom of God and to honour the One who called him to a higher purpose: 'I am an apostle [ambassador] to the Gentiles.'[6] Accepting the call and the challenge to be God's emissary is what catapults us into the grand adventure.[7] It requires a new way of thinking, a change of perspective.

Do not conform to the pattern of this world, but be transformed by the renewing of your mind. Then you will be able to test and approve what God's will is – his good, pleasing and perfect will.
(Rom. 12:2, italics mine)

In the hippie church I attended during the Jesus movement, we loved to quote, 'Do not conform to the pattern of this world.' It's no surprise that this was in our DNA before the rebirth. However, the process of renewing our minds took us a lot further than a radical stance against public policy and expectations.

We were readjusting ourselves and our mindset every day as we prayed, studied God's word, and moved onto the streets with the message of salvation.[8] We were learning how to be ambassadors of the kingdom, reeling in humanity, and becoming the voice and will of God in our community. This is what Jesus was teaching Paul and every believer who holds a passport to his kingdom.[9] Becoming an active, Holy Spirit-led ambassador is an awesome vocation. These are the people we read about in Christian biographies and in the Bible. Their exploits inspire and amaze us. The life of an ambassador has its challenges, but it's never boring. There are two distinct features that mark this life.

- First, ambassadors don't speak for themselves; they speak for, and represent the sovereign who commissioned them.
- Second, ambassadors don't look to the country of their assignment to hand them a pay cheque. All their needs are met by the country that sent them and the ruler they represent.

Of course, being an ambassador of God and his kingdom makes this role even more challenging, but remember, it's not about us; it's about him living in and through us. It's making the unseen tangible, the concealed noticeable, and the will of God witnessed and evidenced in our lives and in this world. My book, *The Kingdom of God: The Director's Cut*, explains this in more depth. May his kingdom come and his will be done on earth as it is in heaven, but it will be through us – not in spite of us.

Kingdom Accountability

Ambassadors don't speak for themselves; they speak for, and represent the sovereign who commissioned them.

Today, many nations grant diplomatic immunity to foreign envoys. This policy stretches back into the ancient world – it's not a modern concept.[1] Diplomacy started the day people decided the message was more important than eating the messenger. Obviously, the report from a neighbouring state could augur life or death, war or peace. Shoot the messenger, and you obscure your future. However, if a state is bent on war, the first person to feel the brunt is usually the resident ambassador.

As Christians, we are accountable to heaven; not to the laws, values and morality of earth. We don't ignore the laws of our resident country; but when they conflict with the principles of God's kingdom, God's will takes priority every time.

The apostles were brought in and made to appear before the Sanhedrin to be questioned by the high priest. 'We gave you strict orders not to teach in this name,' he said. 'Yet you have filled Jerusalem with your teaching and are determined to make us guilty of this man's blood.'

Peter and the other apostles replied: 'We must obey God rather than human beings!'

(Acts 5:27–9)

We need a God-aligned boldness to brazenly stand in the authority of heaven as it contradicts and challenges the establishments of earth. If we don't love what God loves and hate what God hates, we won't even enter into the conversation.

The closer we get to God, the more we delight in love. The more we delight in love, the more we esteem the values of God's kingdom. The deeper our devotion to the king and the kingdom, the sharper the focus – this world is not my home. I'm living in a strange, hostile, foreign land, and I represent a sovereign who is not of this planet, and I speak for him – not myself.

> Very truly I tell you, no servant is greater than his master, *nor is a messenger greater than the one who sent him.*
>
> *(John 13:16, italics mine)*

The disciples (ambassadors) didn't find it any easier to stand against the tide than we do today. So they made it a matter of prayer. They knew a mask energized by self-will and determination wouldn't be enough.

> Now, Lord, consider their threats and enable your servants to speak your word with great boldness.
>
> *(Acts 4:29)*

The disciples knew they needed power from heaven to complete the task assigned to them. The willpower born and propagated on earth will never sustain the people of the kingdom. A supernatural assignment requires supernatural support because our stance challenges not only the people we stand in front of but also the spirits that are often driving them.[2]

This was a brutal lesson for Peter, especially after he denied Jesus three times in one night.[3] We tend to retreat when the fear of death and rejection shout louder than the love of God in our hearts. If we love God, we will speak for him, not just about him. This is what differentiates knowledge from the presence of God.

Even the devil and atheists can talk about the Bible, and in many seminaries, colleges and universities, this is what sometimes happens. This is the curriculum and the goal for the degree but, in God's eyes, this is just the launching pad. We can live in and venerate the wisdom of this world like the ancient Greeks, who made knowledge and wisdom into a science, but the wisdom of God comes with his presence. Jesus is the wisdom of God.[4] God is looking for people who will speak for him and not just about him. This is what it means to be an ambassador of heaven.

Many left Jesus because he boldly and faithfully spoke the words of his Father without compromise.[5] He honoured the God of heaven, not the gods of this world.

> Do you have the gift of speaking? Then speak as though God himself were speaking through you.
>
> *(1 Pet. 4:11, NLT)*

> We are therefore Christ's ambassadors, as though God were making *his* appeal *through* us.
>
> *(2 Cor. 5:20, italics mine)*

God's ambassadors don't represent themselves. Ambassadors don't speak for themselves. They speak for the ruler and the country that commissioned them – the country that issued their passports. They live before an audience of One, the

Creator of heaven and earth. They do not give their opinion or manipulate the message to empower their observations.

The truth of God is not static information. It's active. It's accomplishing something. It will set the captives free and send the demons running. Declare the gospel, and all heaven backs you; water it down, and the devils laugh at our pitiful attempts to be wise and relevant to the world.

The ethics of our community do not inform or direct the morality of God, no matter how logical, expedient and wise it seems in the eyes of the world. The wisdom of this earth is not of God.[6] Jesus didn't go about giving his own opinion regarding the kingdom, and neither should we. As ambassadors, we don't have that authority.

> For I did not speak on my own, but the Father who sent me commanded me to say all that I have spoken. I know that his command leads to eternal life. So whatever I say is just what the Father has told me to say.
>
> *(John 12:49–50)*

> When you are brought before synagogues, rulers and authorities, do not worry about how you will defend yourselves or what you will say, for the Holy Spirit will teach you at that time what you should say.
>
> *(Luke 12:11–12)*

One day a college student came up and asked me what God thought about drugs. Then the conversation turned towards God's outlook on gays, gender, and LGBT issues. As the young man spoke, I noticed another student loitering nearby. I looked at her and said, 'Sorry, I didn't see you there. Do you want something?'

She said, 'No, I'm just interested in the conversation.' That morning, the three of us had a long discussion about God and the moral issues of the day.

To be honest, if it weren't for the Bible and the love of Jesus Christ, I wouldn't really care what drugs they did in private or their sexual orientation. However, I couldn't tell them what they wanted to hear. I am not called to affirm or comfort people in their lifestyles. I represent God and can speak only from God's perspective, not mine. Even though I sensed God's love and concern for these two young people and wanted them to go away feeling affirmed and empowered, I could speak only the words of God. I am only the messenger. It's not about me; it's about his thoughts and his will – not mine. God can speak his own mind better than I, so I just read from the Bible.

> Do not be deceived: neither the sexually immoral nor idolaters nor adulterers nor men who have sex with men nor thieves nor the greedy nor drunkards [drugs] nor slanderers nor swindlers will inherit the kingdom of God.
>
> *(1 Cor. 6:9–10)*

Sexual immorality, impurity and debauchery; idolatry and witchcraft; hatred, discord, jealousy, fits of rage, selfish ambition, dissensions, factions and envy; drunkenness [drugs], orgies, *and the like*. I warn you, as I did before, that those who live like this will not inherit the kingdom of God.

(Gal. 5:19–21, italics mine)

These two students were hoping I would rubber-stamp their lifestyle, but I couldn't do that. I was free to tell them how much God loved them, but I wasn't free to affirm their proclivity towards drugs or their sexual orientation. I also told them the good news of Jesus Christ. They were silent and respectful when they left. I commend them for that. Usually, if someone hates the message, they will also hate the messenger. This world is not my friend, but by the grace of God, I will love everyone in it.

As an ambassador, I'm not allowed to condone what God condemns. The world will promote and applaud those who stand up and celebrate a lifestyle society chooses to approve; I would expect nothing less. As an ambassador of heaven, I can only promote and applaud what has the approval of God. I choose to celebrate God's word and the kingdom values that drive it – on earth as it is in heaven.

I can't compromise God's design and plan for humanity: one man, one woman, then marriage, then sex, then children, and fidelity. I am not allowed to stray from this if I want to stay true to the one who saved me from this world and set me free. Ambassadors cannot allow themselves to be reassimilated into a system God hates.

Do not love the world or anything in the world. If anyone loves the world, love for the Father is not in them. For everything in the world – the lust of the flesh, the lust of the eyes, and the pride of life – comes not from the Father but from the world. The world and its desires pass away, but whoever does the will of God lives for ever.

(1 John 2:15–17)

Often times, when prophets, disciples, apostles, and followers of Jesus (the ambassadors of God) stand up and relay the message of heaven, they are shut down and martyred.[1] The gods of this world hate it when the Creator has something to say on their so-called patch of ground. Jesus warned that this would be an occupational hazard.

If the world hates you, keep in mind that it hated me first. If you belonged to the world, it would love you as its own. As it is, you do not belong to the world, but I have chosen you out of the world. That is why the world hates you. Remember what I told you: 'A servant is not greater than his master.' If they persecuted me, they will persecute you also.

(John 15:18–20)

Being true to God in a crowd of people who are led and deceived by the gods of this world is not easy or safe. It takes courage, boldness and strength from the Holy Spirit in us to stand up and speak up, or to authentically live the life God called us to on this planet. Our lives should be a living expression of heaven on earth. This is why Paul instructs us to put on the full armour of God. Ambassadors need backbone. Timidity is not a fruit of the Spirit. The book of Revelation tells us the first on the list of losers are the cowardly – those who crumble, draw back and recant at the first sign of rejection or persecution.[2]

Stephen's speech to the high priest and the Jewish leaders was bold and courageous.[3] He knew the danger, but he loved Jesus enough to stand his ground as an ambassador of heaven. At the end of a long oration tracing the history of the Jewish people, Stephen concludes with these cutting words.

> You stiff-necked people! Your hearts and ears are still uncircumcised. You are just like your ancestors: you always resist the Holy Spirit! Was there ever a prophet your ancestors did not persecute? They even killed those who predicted the coming of the Righteous One. And now you have betrayed and murdered him – you who have received the law that was given through angels but have not obeyed it.
>
> *(Acts 7:51–3)*

Stephen was doing well until he kicked the hornet's nest. He could have omitted that last paragraph and walked away free, but he was representing God – not himself. This got him killed, but he lost nothing. The people who stoned him were led by Saul the Pharisee. Stephen prays that God will forgive his executioners. Two chapters later, God miraculously confronts Saul, the slayer. He knocks him off his horse, blinds him, and then saves him. He is now the Apostle Paul.

Paul is the answer to Stephen's prayer. Stephen's life was cut short, but his spiritual legacy continued on through the Apostle Paul. Ironically, as Paul said, 'In all things God works for the good of those who love him, who have been called according to his purpose.'[4]

Jesus said those who are faithful in little will be faithful in much.[5] This principle is true. I know sincere people who question whether they would stand up in the face of persecution. This is what I usually advise them.

If you are promoting Jesus now in the little things, don't worry. God's grace will help you stand when it is a matter of life and death. If you are on a path of cowardice and disobedience when God calls you to stand or speak up, then you probably won't change when the stakes are higher. Prepare yourself to rise above your fear and timidity now. Pray for boldness. Step out and face your fear. Don't quench the Spirit or hide your faith.[6] God is with you. Courage doesn't let fear have the last word. Remember, you can't fatten the calf on the day of the sale, faithful in little now, faithful in much later on.

In this world, Christians are facing some heavy persecution. Some of them recant; these are the ones no one talks about or remembers. Others stand their ground for Jesus. These people are awesome.[7] The darker it gets, the brighter their light. If people don't listen to or accept the truth of God, we will be persecuted. If we remain silent, we may escape the world's condemnation, but we won't escape God. As Jesus warned his disciples, 'Do not be afraid of those who kill the body but cannot kill the soul. Rather, be afraid of the One who can destroy both soul and body in hell.'[8]

Whoever acknowledges me before others, I will also acknowledge before my Father in heaven. But whoever disowns me before others, I will disown before my Father in heaven.

(Matt. 10:32–3)

Accepting and taking on the mantle of an ambassador has both its perks and dangers. Jesus was no coward. He boldly embraced the cross; he calls us to do the same.[9] We are like him when we share in his suffering.[10] Trust God. By faith, we put on Christ. Put on the armour of God, and then saddle up and seize the day (*carpe diem*). We have a divine invitation to join the adventure. It's fuelled by love, fraught with danger, invigorated through risk, powered by joy, and driven by the Holy Spirit in us. Being awesome every day is the divine challenge.

Ambassadors don't look to the country of their assignment to hand them a pay cheque. All their needs are met by the country that sent them and the ruler they represent.

Early on in my Christian life, I noticed the signature on my pay cheque was not of this world. Sometimes it was minimum wage, other times it arrived with a bonus, but it was always enough.

One day, as a new Christian, I had paid my bills and was left with 10 dollars. I went to the gas station and put it in the tank so I could get to work the following week. As I stood at the pump, I was thinking, 'Well, this is no fun. Here it is Saturday morning, and I'm already broke.' After I left the station, I went to a bookstore just to look around. While I stood in the aisle, someone walked by and slipped something in my hand and just as quickly walked away. It was a 10-dollar bill. I didn't even pray for it, but God saw my heart. He was teaching me, 'I see you. I know your needs before you ask. I am your source, not this world.'

That same year, I went to the evening service at the hippie church I attended. Again, I was financially embarrassed. Just before the service started, someone came up and gave me 5 dollars without saying a word. Did I look poor? As the collection plate came around, I felt God nudging me to give the 5 dollars to the church, so I said goodbye to the fiver. Again, my pockets were empty. However, after the service, a woman came up to me and put a small box in my hand and said, 'This week I felt God telling me I should give this to you.' I took it home that evening and opened it. It was a diamond ring. It was valued at 900 dollars. Again, God was teaching me. 'I see you. I am your source, not this world.'

A few years later, I couldn't find any work. After a month, I gave up trying. As you know, benefits in the States aren't as extravagant as they are in the United Kingdom. So I went into my room and prayed.

> Father, I've tried and tried, but I can't find a job. I'm tired of looking, so if you agree, this is what I want to do. I will work for you. I will work for free. Wherever there is a need: in the church, for the elderly, painting houses, cleaning, mowing lawns – whatever. I am at your service. I will no longer look to anyone other than you to meet my needs, only you. I will come to you with my request, and no one else will be informed. This will be our secret. If this is acceptable, this is the way I will live. Thank you, Father. Amen.[1]

For a season, God was on this. During those months, I worked for free, but no one knew I was actually working for the Almighty. I was trusting him for my pay cheque. One day I was kneeling in my room and asked the Lord for a new pair of shoes – something I could jog in. A few days later, a friend approached me with his hands behind his back and asked me a rather random question.

'Heh, Richard, what size shoe do you wear?'

'Size twelve. Why do you ask?'

'I just bought a pair of size twelve running shoes that were on sale, two for one. Would you like a pair?'

Whoa! Coincidence? I don't think so. God took me up on my offer, and we were walking this path together. During those months I always had enough money to pay the rent, and there was always food on the table: nothing extravagant but always enough.

During that period of time, I needed some socks. So again I went to my room and asked God for some black ones. A few days later, an acquaintance in the church came by and asked me if I could use some black socks. What can I say? He handed me a good-sized bag of them. They were even washed! I gratefully received them.

I never told him or anyone else of my prayer or the pact I made with my heavenly Father. This is what made it fun – an adventure of faith. It was something personal and special between me and Jesus. The Holy Spirit was guiding and igniting.

I was also learning that prayers need to be specific. If our prayer isn't precise, how will we know if God has answered it? The Almighty wants to make himself known to us, but we need to give him space to do it. A lot of prayers are lost in the ether because of ambiguity. How can we thank God for answering our prayer if our request is vague and obscure? Let God be awesome – be explicit.

Come September, I needed a new winter coat. I was getting the hang of this prayer thingy, so again I went to my room. I thought, I might as well pray for one I really like. 'Lord, could I receive a blue and beige winter jacket? Thank you.' That week I received a brand-new blue and beige jacket. A friend purchased it for me when he went to buy one for himself. I never told him that I asked God for it. This was still a secret between me and God.

After about four months, I was offered a job at a Christian company called Ultimate Support Systems. They made stands for the music industry; they treated their employees well. Again I went to my room and asked God if I should accept permanent employment or continue on the path I was on. This is what I believe he told me.

Take the job. This is also my provision, but remember, I sign the cheques even though they come through your employer. You are working for me. You will never have to concern yourself with provision in this world again. Just keep your eyes and faith focused on me, the kingdom you represent, and the King you serve.

Heaven's Income

This is the story of Donegore Hill and the Moat Inn – our House of Prayer. My wife and I visited the house when I retired from pastoring a church in Belfast. We had no intention to relocate; we viewed it because it was old and interesting. It was built around 1740, and many of the early features were still intact. As the owner led us from room to room, I kept hearing the Lord say, 'My blessing is here. I will bless you here. My blessing is here. I will bless you here.'

I couldn't shake it. When we got back into the car, I blurted out, 'We have to sell our house and buy this place.' The car almost landed in the hedge. When we arrived home, I went to my room and began to write down what I felt God was telling me.

> Don't let anyone talk you out of buying this place. Stay straight on the path. You will sell your house for an x-amount of money. I will bless you there. I will hold on to you there. There will be no sorrow in the gift or turning back from what I want to do among you. It will be a place of healing and ministry for my name's sake. Trust me. Now is the time, something new from something old. Rejoice because I see you and know you and will glorify my name through you. You are mine, and you belong to no one else. Rest and be at peace. I know how to steer your heart, and I have not led you astray.

Now, you may think this sounds very subjective, but on Christmas Eve our house went on the market. Two weeks later we sold it for the exact amount of money God had told me and bought the Moat Inn. That was awesome, but it was just the beginning. Throughout this season of adventure, God kept showing me who was signing the pay cheque. I had got to a place where I didn't even have to pray or ask anymore. All I had to do was abide in Jesus. Put him on. Listen and follow. This is the lifestyle of God's ambassadors.

When we moved in, we needed a large rug to cover the floorboards in the library, and we couldn't find one. We weren't thinking of ourselves; we were thinking of our guests. That week, we were visiting friends and, as we were leaving, they asked, 'We have a rug we wish to give away. Do you want it?' The fact that it was the perfect colour and quality didn't surprise us. So we rolled it up, put it in the car, and drove home.

I was making a 10-foot, black, refectory-type table for the dining room. The room had a simple monastic feel to it. As I was sanding it down, I thought it would be cool to have ten different-styled oak chairs to set around it. That week, we visited some other friends. They knew nothing about the table, but God was ready to do his thing. At the end of our visit, they said, 'We have some old, oak chairs in the garage we need to get rid of; would you like them?' There were ten of them. Coincidence? No way. We hold the passport to heaven, not this earth. Our pay cheque is signed from above.

We had eighteen pastors booked to come on Monday. A week earlier, I was converting our stone garage into a prayer chapel. I was challenged to finish it before they arrived so we could dedicate it to the Lord. As I was painting the rafters, I was thinking how atmospheric it would be to have an old pew along one of the white stone walls. An hour later, a neighbour

I hadn't met before came by and asked me over for a cup of tea. I needed a break, so I went.

You know the drill – God has his ways. At the end of our visit, my neighbour randomly asked, 'Would you be interested in an old pew? We have one we no longer want or need. Take it if you want it.' Of all the things they could have given me, they offered the one object I had been thinking about an hour earlier. They weren't mind-readers, but God sure is.

Regrettably I had no way to get it to my converted chapel. It was 12 feet long. So I climbed the ladder and continued painting the rafters. A while later, a friend from the church arrived for a visit. I mentioned the story about the miracle pew sitting down the road, which prompted the surprising response, 'I have my forklift outside in the truck. I'll go down and get it for you.' Within four hours of thinking about that pew, there it was, sitting along the wall of that little chapel. I'm smiling as I write this – God is exciting, and he is good. On Monday morning eighteen pastors stood and dedicated the prayer space to the Lord and his purposes.

What I find astounding is that I didn't even have to pray or ask God for any of these random objects: a house on a hill, a rug, ten oak chairs and a pew. To me that was awesome. God was way ahead of me and let me know without a doubt that he's the one signing my pay cheque.

During my final year at the Nazarene Theological College in Manchester, England, I ordered some books from the college bookstore. I didn't know what they would cost since they were being purchased from the States. A few weeks later, the librarian informed me they had arrived, and she would like me to come in and pay for them. My finances didn't work out the way I had planned, and I was running on empty – as most students are.

Embarrassed and feeling like a fool, I walk to the bookstore with the note. It was burning a hole in my hand. Who in their right mind orders a pile of theological books without money in the bank? Duh!

The bookstore was a short distance from my dorm room. Slowly, in penitence, I dawdled towards the guillotine. In my mind, I was crawling uphill on my hands and knees over rocks and gravel, wearing a horsehair shirt, and mentally flailing myself with a whip. My inner dialogue was wretched: 'Fool, fool, help, fool, what am I going to say?' At that moment, I felt far from awesome, but when God revealed his hand, I was awed.

I had braced myself to enter the dark cave and face my dragon; but little did I know God was watching my back. Halfway to the bookstore, a student, who I barely knew, came up to me with an envelope. I saw my name on it as he slid it into my hand. I thanked him and returned to my room. Sometimes, procrastination can be a timely, beautiful diversion – a small salute to those who are about to die.

At my desk, I open the gift and read the note. 'Richard, I know this is an odd amount of money, but I believe God told me to give it to you.'

Once again, I felt like Rees Howells at the train station. I was now holding £222. All I could say was, 'Thank you, Lord. You are so good, and thank you to those who listen to your voice and follow your promptings.'

My procrastination flew out of the window like a dove set free from the deck of the ark – or even the *Titanic*. I was now dancing and couldn't wait to pay my bill. With childish glee, I was grinning all the way to the bookstore.

I asked the librarian how much I owed her. She hadn't added it up yet, so I waited as she assessed the list with her calculator. When she finished, she handed it to me and said that it would come to £222.

I almost fell out of my chair. The friend who gave me the money knew nothing about these books. The librarian hadn't even known the cost of them when I stepped through the door. I decided to tell her what had just transpired on my way there. She was flabbergasted and exclaimed, 'That was a miracle.'

I just nodded my head and agreed. 'Yes, it is!'

That day I left the bookstore with a box of new commentaries to help me in my studies and future life ministry. I didn't do anything but dig a hole and jump in it, but I was seeking God's kingdom and his righteousness all the way down.

I have learned over the years that, in spite of my failings, God is watching over me. I am not of this world, and I have the passport to prove it. The signature on my pay cheque is awesome. This is the mindset of an ambassador of Christ. It's an adventure. It's dangerous, but it's so rewarding.

The opportunities to step out in faith and walk on water are constantly set before us. God often tests our hearts to see how far we will go with him.[1] The choice is ours. God is not impeding us. He's clearing the way. He desires to demonstrate his awesomeness through us and to rejoice in our joy as we continue to look to him as our heavenly Father and follow his beloved son, Jesus Christ, our Saviour.

> So do not worry, saying, 'What shall we eat?' or 'What shall we drink?' or 'What shall we wear?' For the pagans run after all these things, and your heavenly Father knows that you need them. But seek first his kingdom and his righteousness, and all these things will be given to you as well. Therefore do not worry about tomorrow, for tomorrow will worry about itself. Each day has enough trouble of its own.
>
> *(Matt. 6:31–4)*

This is the deal Jesus sets before us. He wants to simplify our lives and free us from all the distractions. He's telling us, 'If you centre your life on me, my kingdom, and my values, I will provide your needs for food, clothing and shelter. I will look after this world's essentials if you will devote yourself to the things of heaven.' This doesn't mean we ignore jobs and careers; it means we put God first and view our employment as God's provision. Employers don't have the final say regarding our morality. We are employed by the Creator of heaven and earth, not the person God aligned to feed us.

We like the arrangement. We find comfort in it, but to actually put it to the test and base our lives on his promise takes it to another level. Earlier, I said I made an arrangement with God regarding provision, but really the arrangement was his – he offered it two thousand years ago. All we have to do is endorse the contract and live the life he laid out for us – put his kingdom and his righteousness before everything else. To live as an ambassador of God is an awesome privilege and a fantastic adventure. It's not for the chosen few. He offers it to every believer who is bold enough to step out of the boat.

'Jesus, can I come out to you on the water?'

'Come!'

'What about the others who are safely sitting in the boat?'

'What is that to you? Follow me!'

As ambassadors, we need to sign on the dotted line. It's the contract God sets before us. It's a tale of two cities. Who will we serve? What passport will we embrace? It's a choice between the kingdom of God and the kingdoms of this world.

PART
FIVE

The Snapshots

32

Look

People ask, 'Where is God? Where's the proof of his exist-ence?' My answer is simple: 'God is here, but you as yet don't have the eyes to see him. God is speaking to us all the time; you just aren't tuned to the right frequency.' Consider this episode in the Gospel of John.

> 'Father, glorify your name!' Then a voice came from heaven, 'I have glorified it, and will glorify it again.' The crowd that was there and heard it said it had thundered; others said an angel had spoken to him.
>
> *(John 12:28–9)*

Hmm, was it thunder or the voice of an angel? Was it a nat-ural phenomenon or a miraculous encounter with heaven? If we had been there that day, would we have been reaching for our umbrellas or rejoicing in the living voice of God? Would we quickly have explained away the occurrence as a natural phenomenon or rejoiced in the revelation?

The Bible calls this kind of deaf-blindness 'hardness of heart'. Pharaoh had it.[1] Half of this crowd experienced it and, surprisingly, even the twelve disciples were victims of it. As a matter of fact, to some extent, we all struggle with hardness of heart. It's a spiritual malady, a handicap God wants to lift from us.

We find this played out in the Gospel of Mark. In Mark 6, Jesus feeds the five thousand. The disciples witnessed the miracle first-hand. They even participate. They touch and carry the food. They look and observe the multiplication. They even pick up the leftovers. That was an awesome event that should have marked an unforgettable, awesome day with the Lord.

That same evening, Jesus walked toward the disciples. They were in the boat, and he was on the water. They didn't recognize him at first. They were terrified and thought he was a ghost.[2] Mark explains the reason for their fear and surprise.

> Immediately he spoke to them and said, 'Take courage! It is I. Don't be afraid.' Then he climbed into the boat with them, and the wind died down. They were completely amazed, for *they had not understood about the loaves; their hearts were hardened.*
>
> *(Mark 6:50–52, italics mine)*

They were amazed that Jesus walked on water because they didn't understand the miracle of the loaves. One stemmed from the other. If they had understood what God had revealed through the feeding of the five thousand, they wouldn't have been afraid when Jesus walked towards them, skimming the waves. Their hearts were hard.

Now let's follow the story and dig a little deeper. In Mark 8, we find Jesus and the disciples in the same situation as when they fed the five thousand back in Mark 6. Mark writes the narrative to mirror what took place in the earlier feeding story. Once more, there is concern about the crowd and their lack of sustenance. Jesus asks the disciples again about the food supply. Again, it was very little – another impossible situation. But heh, the disciples should be on it, shouldn't they? I can imagine Peter comforting Thomas.

Don't worry, brother. In chapter six, we fed five thousand with just a few fish and loaves. This crowd is smaller. It's only four thousand. This will be a walk in the park. Aren't we old hands at this multiplication wonder? Exert some faith.

Then he would look over at the sons of thunder. They were biting at the bit to call down fire from heaven.

Cool it, boys. We're here to give them bread, not toast.

Then Judas the treasurer skulks up to Peter, bouncing the money bag in his left hand as he whispers.

You know, Peter, if we charged three shekels a head, financially we could keep this discipleship programme going for another three years.

Is this facetious? Yes, but wouldn't you expect some level of faith, excitement and anticipation among these chosen disciples? Wouldn't you jump at the chance to repeat the miracle? I would, but listen to their lame response after Jesus explains the situation.

'I have compassion for these people; they have already been with me three days and have nothing to eat. If I send them home hungry, they will collapse on the way, because some of them have come a long distance.'

His disciples answered, 'But where in this remote place can anyone get enough bread to feed them?'

(Mark 8:2–4)

What? Are you serious? Men of faith? They act as though the previous feeding miracle never happened. To them, it appears to have been a one-off event, quickly forgotten. This is what a hard heart looks like and the way it behaves – deaf and blind. A person with a hard heart has difficulty connecting all the dots. So Jesus administers the remedy. He goes through each step as he did before when he fed the five thousand. He takes the bread. He blesses it. He gives it to the disciples to pass around. Then again, he tells them to collect the leftovers.[3] He repeats each step because he's trying to pry open the eyes and ears of the disciples to hear the voice of God and to recognize the divine fingerprints he leaves behind. What's all this pointing to? What is God saying through all of this activity? Did they learn anything? Are their hearts still hard? Let's read on.

Just before Jesus gets into the boat with the disciples, after feeding this second crowd, he has a brief encounter with the Pharisees.[4] This sets the scene for what happens next. Mark informs us that the disciples were short of food, and they assume Jesus is worried that they won't have enough to feed themselves – crazy.

> The disciples had forgotten to bring bread, except for one loaf they had with them in the boat. 'Be careful,' Jesus warned them. 'Watch out for the yeast of the Pharisees and that of Herod.'
>
> They discussed this with one another and said, 'It is because we have no bread.'
>
> Aware of their discussion, Jesus asked them: 'Why are you talking about having no bread? Do you still not see or understand? *Are your hearts hardened? Do you have eyes but fail to see, and ears but fail to hear? And don't you remember?* When I broke the five loaves for the five thousand, how many basketfuls of pieces did you pick up?'

'Twelve,' they replied.

'And when I broke the seven loaves for the four thousand, how many basketfuls of pieces did you pick up?'

They answered, 'Seven.'

He said to them, 'Do you still not understand?'

(Mark 8:14–21, italics mine)

In this short episode, Jesus tells us what hardness of heart actually is. 'Hardness of heart' is having all the faculties to listen but not hearing; it's having the power of sight but not seeing. It's living in the physical world with our spiritual antennas turned off. Hardness of heart simply points to a lack of spiritual perception. The Lord could speak from heaven in an audible voice, but a person with a hard heart only hears meaningless rumbles because the voice doesn't fit into their world-view.

Jesus knew his disciples would never fulfil the mission if their hearts were hard. If we can't see or hear the voice of God or recognize his fingerprints, then how can we follow the leading of the Holy Spirit? God didn't just give us a book of instructions; he gave us his risen Son and his Holy Spirit. The Holy Spirit is alive in us. The Holy Spirit is not asleep or dormant. The Spirit is not a silent resident loitering about in our hearts, waiting for the second coming. We don't have to wake him up. We are the ones who need to stir and open our ears and eyes to what is going on around us.

So as we just read, Jesus asked the disciples a few logistical questions about the leftovers. Why did he do this? It's because he wanted them to think about the miracles and not forget them. Meditate on them. Start asking the right questions. Pray about them. What does this series of events imply? What is this sign pointing to?

This is how God gets us to open our spiritual eyes and ears to understand and recognize the fingerprints of God and what he's touching and communicating at the moment – how to read and follow the eternity-microchip-tracker God has implanted in the human heart. Jesus wants all his disciples to move beyond the deeds and understand the ways of God, as did Moses.[5]

So in faith we sign up for God's discipleship programme. The principal lesson is to readjust our reality gauge. Expect more from God. Look around and believe he is revealing himself in and through our circumstances, especially in the recurring patterns and seasons of life we find ourselves in. God is making himself known. If we don't believe God is communicating with us, we won't bother to tune into his frequency. It's difficult to hear the voice of God if we don't believe he is speaking to us.

You will be pleased to know that the disciples finally got the message. I like happy endings. One paragraph later, Jesus asks, 'Who do you say I am?'

Peter answers, 'You are the Messiah.'[6]

Jesus congratulates and honours Peter because his eyes were finally opened. The disciples were beginning to see and recognize the fingerprints of God. They were looking beyond the deeds and seeing God's ways, how God communicates, and how God reveals himself.

> Blessed are you, Simon son of Jonah, for this was not revealed to you by flesh and blood, but by my Father in heaven.
>
> *(Matt. 16:17)*

At last, they opened themselves up enough to get it. This is what Jesus was working towards in all these events. If we want to be awesome for Jesus in this world, if we thirst for the kingdom adventure, we need eyes to see and ears to hear – we need to be spiritually tuned in and turned on.[7] Open our eyes, Lord; we want to see Jesus. Open our ears, Lord; we want to hear your voice, not the distant thunder that echoes in our heads. Reaching for an umbrella when God speaks is about as awesome as the cheeseburger accolades I read on Facebook. I don't believe any of us wants to look back on our lives and exclaim, 'Surely the LORD is in this place, and I was not aware of it.'[8]

> Earth's crammed with heaven,
> And every common bush afire with God,
> But only he who sees takes off his shoes;
> The rest sit round and pluck blackberries.
>
> *Elizabeth Barrett Browning*

33

Listen

Hearing the voice of God is a sticky subject. Many killers have blamed their criminal activity on divine transmissions – but that's the extreme. However, we Christians should also be wary of climbing over the side of the boat when Jesus isn't standing there beckoning us onto the water. The voice we hear is not always the voice we claim, but that doesn't discount divine communication from the Holy Spirit. Delusion is rampant when people, Christian and otherwise, try to tune into the voice of God before they know and understand the ways of God revealed in his written word.[1]

Personally, I believe God is speaking all the time, especially to those who have faith to listen and ears to hear. God didn't give us a book and then hang up the phone. We have been invited into a divine love relationship. His goal is not to populate the new heaven and the new earth but to cultivate intimacy with us. He desires passionate interaction founded on love and adoration. This is why God, the Holy Spirit, lives within us.[2] How intimate is that?[3]

We are the bride of Christ, not just the saved.[4] Not that he desires or needs our scintillating conversation but, like a father with a child, he wants to embrace and communicate with us personally. Many times, it is through his written word that he speaks directly to our hearts. That's when the Bible becomes personal – a revelation that takes the words on a page and breathes life into them. This is the main way God intimately communicates with us, but it's not the only way he speaks. However, what he does say will always be in line with his character as revealed in the Bible. It is just as important to know *who* is being communicated, as *what* is being said. Is the message in line with his words and his nature?

Like us, God has various ways to transmit his thoughts. We have our phones, emails, letters in the post, and the social media exchange. God speaks through Scripture, nature, messengers, dreams, visions, and insightful pictures that flash across the brain – which I would call a stagnant vision. Many of these require interpretation – an ongoing revelation and explanation from the Holy Spirit. Then there is that colourful, mysterious still, small voice Elijah heard on Mount Horeb.[5] Rabbinic Judaism calls this divine, disembodied whisper the *bat kol*: the daughter of a voice.

I don't see visions or have divinely inspired dreams that I am aware of, but I believe I hear God's words. I communicate with him through language, and I receive from him through language. That is the way I am wired. This is what I mean when I talk about listening and hearing the voice of God. Have you ever walked down the street and sensed that inner voice prompting you to go over and speak to that person by the bus stop?

Often, we question the validity of those thoughts: 'Oh, that's just me; that's not God.' Then the message takes root and doesn't let up. We try to ignore the thought and brush it away. We even feel guilty because we didn't act on it. Believe me, that was probably the voice of God speaking to us, but we didn't want to do it. We just ran away like Jonah. The more we spurn the voice of God, the more challenging it is to hear him. We aren't born with hard hearts; we cultivate them. Here are some thoughts that have helped me distinguish the voice of God from all the others.

First, God's voice sounds like our voice. God speaks to us through the Holy Spirit, who dwells within us. The words of God come to our spirit before they reach our minds. Our spirit then triggers them in our heads; this is why the voice of God often sounds like our own. Consider these words of the Apostle Paul:

> The Spirit searches all things, even the deep things of God. For who knows a person's thoughts except their own spirit within them? In the same way no one knows the thoughts of God except the Spirit of God. What we have received is not the spirit of the world, but the Spirit who is from God . . . we have the mind of Christ.
>
> *(1 Cor. 2:10–16)*

Second, the voice of God carries an authority we don't possess. So I've learned that when a thought prompts questions like, 'Was that God or me?' it most likely was God, or we wouldn't have bothered to ask the question in the first place. We don't usually scrutinize the origin of our own thoughts. Such questions arise because of the authority of God behind his words.

Now, I'm not saying that every time that question is asked, it automatically bona fides the message and gives it the divine stamp of approval. All I'm saying is that if it lines up with the Bible, the character and the ways of God, then it is most likely him speaking to us – even though it sounds like our own voice.

Third, we will never really know if it's God until we step out and test it. Back in the early eighties, I was at a Christian conference when a woman sat down next to me. Through the entire programme, I sensed God whisper, 'The woman next to you wishes she was a man.' I just quietly sat there.

As the conference came to a close, I felt God nudging me to tell her what he said. Now, that may have been a tad easier in today's climate than it was forty years ago, but I wanted to be sensitive to the voice of God, so I told her, 'I believe God is saying you wish you were a man instead of a woman.' Then I braced myself for the backlash – it didn't come.

Her response surprised me. She said that was exactly what she was thinking, but it had nothing to do with sex or gender. Her angst had to do with ministerial opportunities in the church she attended. She said men were permitted to do everything but not the women. We talked and prayed together. I believe, if anything, she at least left knowing God is watching over her and is pleased about her desire to serve him.

I don't always get it right, but I will never know if it is God or not until I test the waters. If I speak in love and get it wrong, I just apologize and admit I'm on a learning curve. I believe God is more pleased that I tried than if I just played it safe and ignored him.

There is a prayer group that meets periodically in my home. We start each meeting by asking God to show us what's on his mind – what does he want us to pray about at that particular moment? Then we wait, listen and then begin. We kneel, we pace the floor, we sit, we worship, and God comes. The point is that we are talking to God while also listening. Many times at the end of our meetings, someone will say, 'Just before you started to pray that, the same thought came to my mind.' Sometimes we would pray about one subject for over an hour because of the leading of the Holy Spirit.

In one meeting, we were praying about the government in Northern Ireland. In the middle of our prayers, I believe I had a download from heaven. It carried authority and stopped me in my tracks. I told my friends I believe God just spoke to me and said, 'The answer for this island is not the government; the answer for this island is the church.' Everyone sensed that it was the voice of God. From there, we focused our prayers on the church and its influence on the nation. For me, this is still a matter of prayer and intercession. However, I find this practice helps to sensitize and alert me to the voice of God. Pray and listen; listen and pray with like-minded people who want to fine-tune their spiritual ears.

During my morning prayer time, I periodically ask God what he wants to say to me. Then I sit at a keyboard or with a pen and paper and start writing. I don't concern myself with punctuation or grammar, and I don't pause to think about what I am going to write down. I just pray, ask, and then write. Some days it's only a paragraph; once in a while, it's almost a full page. I write as though God is speaking directly to me. Sometimes it's very general. 'Trust me, son. I am with you.' Sometimes it is specific and even prophetic. 'You will sell your house for this specific amount of money.'[6]

Now, I know this kind of exercise can be a mixture of God's voice and my own, but that's OK. I don't believe I ever write outside of God's will or character, and at times I find myself writing things I have never thought of before. This is not automatic writing. It's just giving God space to speak.

Jesus told us that hearing the voice of God is part of the normal Christian life. If we aren't listening and obeying, we will rarely experience those awesome God moments to tell our children or the next generation, and that is a tragedy.[7]

My sheep listen to my voice; I know them, and they follow me.
(John 10:27)

One Sunday morning, after I stepped down from the pulpit, my young son excitedly darted around the church, announcing, 'We're going to Las Vegas!' In a denomination that wouldn't promote gambling, this required some explanation – my mother lives there.

For over twenty-five years, we visited Vegas to see my mother. As a family, we've never dropped a coin in a slot machine; we're boring that way. We try to behave even when no one is watching – you know, live before an audience of One. However, it's always a gamble to decipher the fingerprints of God around us and then act on them. We don't always get it right, but I sure don't want to close down and harden my heart out of fear. Where's the adventure in that?

Each time we visit Vegas, I usually get up early and go for a long walk before the sun gets hot. One morning, when I was passing through a neighbourhood, I sensed the Holy Spirit upon me. I prayed for the families living in that area, and I thanked God for his goodness. Two days later, in that same neighbourhood, I had a second Holy Spirit encounter. That's when I started to question God. This is what you do if you don't want a hard heart. I prayed about it because, in all the years I had spent on that path, I had never sensed the Holy Spirit so active and strong there. This was something new to me, and I couldn't shake it off.

That Sunday, we visited a local church. I ended up having a long conversation with one of the elders. I told him of my recent experience in their neighbourhood and what I felt God was saying.

> I believe the Spirit of God is hovering over your community right now and is ready to act. It's an answer to your prayers. The Holy Spirit hovered over the waters in Genesis, but nothing happened until God spoke. The Holy Spirit is now hovering over your community, waiting for God's people to step out, probably in a way you have never done before, and reap the harvest. Seek him while he can be found. Call upon him while he is near. Step out because the way is open – right now. Don't let this opportunity pass you by.

After I said this, he told me he had goose bumps up and down his arms. I believe that was the Holy Spirit confirming the message to him. After I arrived home that afternoon, I started to pray for the elders of that church. I was also praying about those goose bumps (I know – you don't need to tell me how crazy this all is).

Then it came to me that God was specifically pointing out that one elder. He was probably the key person God wanted to work through. This was a divine encounter, and I apologized to God for not telling that man he was the person God was calling to step up to the task. So I prayed, 'Lord, if you want me to speak to that person about this, make a way. Let me meet him again.'

The next day, there he was, standing in the parking lot of the grocery store – surprise, surprise! We continued the conversation we had started on the Sunday morning. I told him what I believed God was saying about him, personally. He listened and thanked me.

I believe I was God's ambassador that day. If anything, I would rather fail by overstepping the mark than fail because my heart was hard and cowardly. Be awesome, every day – heh! Sometimes we get it right, sometimes we don't, but woe to those who never try.

Most of the time, God is communicating with us. If we ignore him, and tune him out, his voice will eventually become an indistinguishable thought buried in the cacophony of our own minds. We will have ears to hear, but we will not hear because we have hardened our hearts to the voice of God.

Each time we disobey, our hearts grow a bit harder. A 'yes' to God opens our hearts; a 'no' to God hardens our hearts. The more we say 'yes' in obedience, the more we nurture our sensitivity to God's ways and the movement of the Holy Spirit. We begin to recognize the fingerprints of God all around us and hear God's voice, even in the thunderstorm. This is the adventure – the awesome life God has invited us to step into.

> Today, if you hear his voice,
>> do not harden your hearts
> as you did in the rebellion,
>> during the time of testing in the wilderness,
> where your ancestors tested and tried me,
>> though for forty years they saw what I did.
> That is why I was angry with that generation;
>> I said, 'Their hearts are always going astray,
>> and they have not known my ways.'

(Heb. 3:7–10)

35

Pray

Inner-city Glasgow is lined with row upon row of sandstone tenement homes. During my time there as an associate pastor, I lived on the top floor of one of those historic buildings. The church was just a few doors down the road. I had two rooms and a small kitchen. The front bay window looked out over a busy crossroads. During the day, those streets and pavements were bustling with people and traffic.[1] From my first morning onward, I would stand at that window, look out and pray, 'Father God, let me see these people as you see them and love them as you love them.' God answered that prayer.

One Sunday, after the evening service, a young woman in her mid-twenties came into the building asking for help. I watched as she paced back and forth in front of me, very agitated, repeating, 'Oh God, help me. Please, God, help me.' Between her cries for help and assistance, she told me of her heroin addiction and how she had overdosed a few times that year. Heroin addiction was rife in that part of the city.

I told her we would pray and, as a church, do everything we could to help her. Then she hurried away, arranging to meet up with me the next day. She never showed up. A few days later, I got a phone call from a nearby pastor.

'Hello, Richard. Do you know Sheryl?'

'Yes, I saw her a few days ago. We arranged to meet up, but she didn't come.'

'She said she knew you. That is why I am calling. I'm sorry to tell you this over the phone, but she's dead. Yesterday evening, she died of an overdose.'

I was stunned. The pastor then asked if I would help officiate at her funeral. Many of Sheryl's friends, family and her 5-year-old son attended. It was the hardest funeral I ever took part in. My heart was breaking, not just for Sheryl, but for all the substance-affected users suffering in the community.

That's when things changed – in me. I could no longer pray. For the next three years, I would stand at my window every morning and weep as I looked out at the people in the streets below. I had no more words. Each time I tried to speak, I was overcome with compassion. I was overwhelmed by the love and concern of God for the people of Glasgow. I'm finding it hard even to write this now without crying. I discovered that when God touches your heart about something, it never goes away.

We are told to pray in the Spirit, but it works on two levels.[2] Prayer is when *we ask through the Holy Spirit*. Intercession is when *the Holy Spirit asks through us*. Prayer is alignment with *the mind of God*. Intercession is in alignment with *the heart of God*.

Interceding is more than just praying for something or someone other than yourself. It's actually putting yourself in their place. It's spiritual empathy. It's taking on someone else's pain, their lostness and their emotional baggage and carrying them all physically and ardently to God. Both Moses and the Apostle Paul took this mantle upon themselves. Their intercessory prayers were quite scary.

Oh, what a great sin these people have committed! They have made themselves gods of gold. But now, please forgive their sin – but if not, then blot me out of the book you have written.

(Exod. 32:31–2)

I speak the truth in Christ – I am not lying, my conscience confirms it through the Holy Spirit – I have great sorrow and unceasing anguish in my heart. For I could wish that I myself were cursed and cut off from Christ for the sake of my people, those of my own race, the people of Israel.

(Rom. 9:1–4)

These are awesome prayers. Would you give up your salvation for your neighbour or the people in your community? Would I? That's a hard question; maybe an unfair one. Intercession is not natural. It only happens when we put on Christ – or when we let Christ put on us.

Isaiah prophesied words that can be easily applied to the coming Messiah. Jesus takes this prophecy and links it to himself and what he is to face on the cross.

He poured out his life unto death,
    and was numbered with the transgressors.
For he bore the sin of many,
    and made intercession for the transgressors.

(Isa. 53:12, italics mine)

It is written: 'And he was *numbered with the transgressors*'; and I tell you that this must be fulfilled in me. Yes, what is written about me is reaching its fulfilment.

(Luke 22:37, italics mine)

On the cross, Jesus said, 'Father, forgive them, for they do not know what they are doing.'[3] Now that is a great prayer. It's full of grace and mercy. But the Bible calls it an intercession, not a prayer – why? If he said this in the comfort of a mid-week prayer meeting, it would be just a prayer – a good prayer. The fact that he was nailed to a cross, carrying the sin of the world on his shoulders, and then carrying the world physically and emotionally to God, his Father, is what made it an intercession. Can you see the difference?

With shattered bones and blood running down his face, Stephen cries out to God, 'Lord, do not hold this sin against them.'[4] If I heard someone say this in the comfort of a prayer meeting, I would be impressed. This too is a great prayer, but what makes it an intercession is that Stephen's asking God to forgive his executioners. The compassion of God moved him beyond any natural response or affection. He was concerned about those who were killing him – he was pleading for their souls in the mercy of God.

However, intercession is more than words or even tears. True intercession compels us to be God's answer to the pleadings of the Holy Spirit through us. In Glasgow, I found those suffering from addictions and their families were on my heart night and day. I would invite them into my home. I listened to their manipulative and often disturbing conversation. I was robbed twice by people who broke into my flat, but I kept bringing them before God, serving them, and sharing with them the love God has for them through Jesus. The church now has active recovery programmes in the community, and many have come to know God.

Prayer is easy, intercession has a price. Intercession is a plunge into the heart of God. There is a lot of praying going on in the church, but where are the intercessors? When we read about the revivals of the past, we begin to see that the revival didn't spark and take off until the prayer meetings became open intercessions. Perhaps a good place for us to begin is with this simple request: 'Oh Lord, help me to see them as you see them and to love them as you love them.' Amen.

In the same way, the Spirit helps us in our weakness. We do not know what we ought to pray for, but the Spirit himself intercedes for us through wordless groans. And he who searches our hearts knows the mind of the Spirit, because the Spirit intercedes for God's people in accordance with the will of God.

(Rom. 8:26–7)

36

Love

God is love. We are to be like God. Every sin is an affront to love. Every spiritual act that isn't grounded in love is a clanging cymbal to the worshipping ears of heaven. Holiness is love in character, action and motivation. Everything Jesus did was born out of compassion. What more can I say? Read between the lines.

> For God so loved the world that he gave his one and only Son, that whoever believes in him shall not perish but have eternal life.
>
> *(John 3:16)*

> Follow God's example, therefore, as dearly loved children and live a life of love, just as Christ loved us and gave himself up for us as a fragrant offering and sacrifice to God.
>
> *(Eph. 5:1–2)*

We welcome the tangible presence of God and show our love for him each time we listen and obey. We welcome his presence each morning as we get dressed from his closet. We welcome his presence when we live as ambassadors of heaven and put on the armour. When we put on Jesus, we put on love, and God covers us in the anointing of his Holy Spirit – in us and upon us. We make a difference on this earth for God, and wild and supernatural encounters take place all around us. We just need the eyes to see and the ears to hear.

Is this normal? Not to the people on the streets, but as ambassadors of another, otherworldly kingdom, this is what normal looks like. It's the resurrection power and life of God, energized and motivated by love. The fruit of the Spirit and the gifts of the Spirit are manifestations of love in all its incarnations.

I will never forget the day I stood in front of a shop in Manchester. My friend was looking for some office supplies. Before we opened the door, he looked through the window and saw some of the posters hanging on the wall. Then he said, 'You know, Richard, I'm not going in there.' I asked him why. His answer floored me. 'I'm not going in there because Jesus is much too precious to me.' Later, he told me he just didn't want those lewd poster images in his head – not because he was a Christian, prudish, or a living saint in religious terms, but because he loved Jesus.

This is the key that unlocks the door to everything explored in the pages of this book. The love of God is the fire that fuels us. It's the unending supply of oil – the everlasting fountain. This is what we were created for – an eternal, intimate, love relationship with our Creator, who is love.

Love is the only motivation that will move us forward and upward. I resist sin because I love Jesus, not because I fear hell. I love people because Jesus loves them – all of them. I desire the gifts of the Holy Spirit because I want people to encounter the reality of God's love. I put on Christ and walk in the fruit of the Holy Spirit because I want to be like Jesus. God is teaching us what love is, what it looks like, and how to live a life motivated by compassion. I trust him to love through me. My warm, gushy feelings are selective; his are all-encompassing. The closer we get to Jesus, the greater our capacity to love. After Peter denied the Lord three times, Jesus didn't ask:

- Peter, will you serve me?
- Peter, do you repent?
- Peter, will you try to do better and not deny me the next time?

- Peter, will you be more courageous?
- Peter, will you follow me?

No, Jesus got right to the heart of the matter. He addressed what concerned him the most. 'Peter, do you love me?' Three times Jesus repeated this question. He was healing Peter's heart and conscience, helping him to overwrite the three failures he carried in his heart and mind. Jesus knew love was the only thing that would motivate and keep Peter steady for the mission. Everything else would be academic and untenable.

What I also find motivating is that each time Peter professed his love for Jesus, he received a directive. It was progressive. 'Feed my lambs.' 'Take care of my sheep.' 'Feed my sheep.' 'Follow me.'[1] It's the Lord's way of saying, 'Love God – love others.' You can't love others until you are secure in the love of and for God. He is the source of love. This is foundational to the life we are called to live. This is what brings heaven to earth – on earth as it is in heaven.

If Jesus were to ask us anything right now or even when we die, he probably wouldn't start with, 'Do you believe in me?' Instead, he would ask the question he asked Peter – the Peter question.

- Do you love me?
- Are you learning how to love?
- Are you allowing me to love others through you?

It's the first commandment. Love is what motivated Jesus when he walked through Israel. If we love him, we will be motivated to obey, listen, serve, pray, worship, and love others.

The *Westminster Shorter Catechism* tells us the chief aim of our existence is to glorify God and enjoy him forever. This was written by a group of English and Scottish theologians in 1646–7. It sounds a lot like worship to me. We gratefully receive the manna, look up and glorify God in the meal.

> So whether you eat or drink or whatever you do, do it all for the glory of God.
>
> *(1 Cor. 10:31)*

If we were worshipping an idol, it would be a one-way street. Idols don't interact with humans or respond to worship, even though it's an open invitation to demons. However, the images just sit there, being pooed on by pigeons and collecting dust. The devotee's worship is singular. They have to stir themselves up and invent new reasons to inspire them. It's a futile exercise – an attempt to draw water from an empty well.

Christian worship isn't like that. It's as intimate as the Holy Spirit living inside of us. We know and sense God's presence. He reveals more of himself, and we rejoice and applaud the revelation. We listen to his voice and obey – this is worship. It's how we honour him.

True worship in spirit and in truth is a life, not just an event. Bring the guitars and kick out the jams; sing the Bible and rejoice. This is great. We do it every Sunday in one form or another, but that is just a worship experience. Anyone can attend and participate in the gathering, but worship takes on a whole new dimension when it becomes a way of life. Worship is a lifestyle, not just a scheduled occurrence. It's a consistent surrender that honours God in everything, every moment, even when things get dark.

We often think our worship will be richer and more honouring to God when we cross the bridge into heaven. In some ways, yes; in other ways, no. Today we have the chance to worship God when we are hurting, confused, bewildered or even suffering loss. This side of eternity offers us opportunities we will never have on the other embankment. John tells us God will wipe away every tear in the new heaven and the new earth.[1] There are no tears in the sweet bye and bye, but there sure are a lot of them here on earth right now.

It's easy to worship when we see God face-to-face, standing with all the saints and angelic host, lifting our hands and bowing with the twenty-four elders, laying crowns before him. There we will be worshipping as the waves of joy, peace and love embrace us. That honours God, but when we lift our heads down here in the midst of all the turmoil, acknowledging his goodness and love in devotion, it elevates worship to a place heaven has hardly experienced. Satan himself never expected us to worship God as we suffered trials and misfortune. This is what lay behind the challenge faced by Job.

> Then the LORD said to Satan, 'Have you considered my servant Job? There is no one on earth like him; he is blameless and upright, a man who fears God and shuns evil.'
>
> 'Does Job fear God for nothing?' Satan replied. 'Have you not put a hedge around him and his household and everything he has? You have blessed the work of his hands, so that his flocks

and herds are spread throughout the land. But now stretch out your hand and strike everything he has, and he will surely curse you to your face.'

(Job 1:8–11)

Nonetheless, Job stood the test.

Naked I came from my mother's womb,
    and naked I shall depart.
The Lord gave and the Lord has taken away;
    may the name of the Lord be praised.

(Job 1:21)

Satan and his cohorts didn't anticipate that response. It was authentic, atomic-powered worship. It was probably unlike anything seen or experienced in the blissful realm of paradise. Satan's view of worship and its motivation is quite shallow, and many on earth, even those who attend church, fulfil his expectations. That day, Job was awesome, even though his wife didn't get it.

His wife said to him, 'Are you still maintaining your integrity? Curse God and die!'

(Job 2:9)

Worship to God is a sacrifice laid on the altar. It's burning hot. It's given willingly. It is a life surrendered to the Almighty. True worship, in the Spirit and in truth, is not just an event – it's a life. Worship is not just something we do, it's everything we do.

Twenty-four-seven worship meetings inspire me. I attended one in Kansas City when I was there.[2] King David[3] instigated one, as did later followers of Jesus.[4] I am always challenged when I read about Anna the prophet: 'She never left the temple but worshipped night and day, fasting and praying.'[5]

However, we don't have to attend a worship service or live in a temple to worship God with our lives. We should always honour God, in our work, at home and even in our relaxation. We don't jump off the altar when we leave the church building or when we stop singing the songs. Everything we have talked about in this book is an act of worship.

> Therefore, I urge you, brothers and sisters, in view of God's mercy, to offer your bodies as a living sacrifice, holy and pleasing to God – this is your true and proper worship.
>
> *(Rom. 12:1)*

I would rather talk about a life of worship than specific events or songs. We worship God when we resist temptation. We are telling God, 'I love you more than I love myself.' Even godly conversation among family and friends is adoration.

> Then those who feared *the LORD talked with each other, and the LORD listened and heard.* A scroll of remembrance was written in his presence concerning those who feared the LORD and honoured his name.
>
> 'On the day when I act,' says the LORD Almighty, 'they will be my treasured possession.'
>
> *(Mal. 3:16–17, italics mine)*

I love this verse. Think about it. God is telling Malachi, 'I overheard this conversation in Israel the other day. The participants didn't know I was there eavesdropping, but I really liked what I heard.' I wonder if our conversations sound like worship to the ears of God. We talk about who and what we love. 'For the mouth speaks what the heart is full of.'[6] Is our worship pleasing to God? Will today's conversations be as pleasing to the ears of God as our Sunday-morning church service?

Religion is sitting in church thinking about the new car. Worship is sitting in the new car and thinking about God. Religion focuses on payback; worship focuses on the glory of God and the love we can reciprocate. It is a surrender without conditions or personal agendas. The more we get to know and love God, the deeper our worship. Our value system aligns with the concerns of heaven and not the cares and worries of earth. We readjust our gaze to the One above. He becomes more real and present than anything this world offers. God alone becomes our goal, our delight and our desire.

Just before stepping into Gethsemane, Jesus prayed, 'I have brought you glory on earth by finishing the work you gave me to do.'[7] That exemplifies a life of worship. We were in God's heart and mind before he said, 'Let there be light.' Becoming what God envisioned us to be, completing everything God informed us to do, and then presenting it all to him with love and gratitude is true worship. It's the legacy we leave behind, but it's also what we take with us. This is what worship in spirit and truth looks like. It follows us into heaven as we surrender and honour the God above and not the gods of this earth: 'Father, into your hands I commit my spirit.'[8] Amen.

Obey

Moses wandered into the desert and encountered God at the burning bush. John the Baptist dwelled in the desert to be close to the Almighty. The Apostle Paul hung out in the desert regions, receiving revelations from Jesus.[1] Early monks trekked into the desert of Egypt to meet with God. In 1983, Richard Porter is dropped off in the desert for ten days to keep his self-appointed engagement with the Lord of heaven and earth. Yee-haw! What a saint!

The Apostle John tells us we love God because he first loved us, and God is the One who initiates our relationship with him through the Holy Spirit. So it might sound a bit presumptuous to say I set up the appointment, but it sure seemed that way.

It was summer, and I had two weeks of holidays coming up. I was single and comfortable in my own company, so I thought I would take my Bible and head out into the wilderness to fast and pray for ten days. This was my appointment. Like John the Baptist or the Apostle Paul, who received revelations in the desert, I was psyching myself up for the pilgrimage. There was no agenda, just a hunger. I wanted to meet with God like the people I read about in the Bible and throughout church history.

My home at the time was in Fort Collins, Colorado, and my destination was Pawnee Buttes. It was approximately 76 miles away, as flat as a kitchen table except for two level-topped hills.

Now when Jesus fasted and prayed in the wilderness, the Bible says, he was also with the wild animals.[2] These animals were dangerous: lions, bears, scorpions and snakes. I knew Pawnee Buttes was riddled with rattlesnakes, so I bought a shepherd's crook to push them away if I accidentally encountered one. My small, one-person tent was always tightly zipped, so they couldn't crawl into my sleeping bag. I came upon two during my stay there, but I kept my distance.

What I didn't know until my first day was that a local farmer had let his bull run free. There were no trees to climb, and if that bull decided I was intruding on its territory, I would be in big trouble. So I always tried to map out the bull's location and keep a good distance between us. Doesn't this sound like fun? However, I had made the appointment, and I wasn't going to miss my rendezvous with the Almighty because of a few inconvenient dangers.

Every day leading up to the retreat, I would often say to myself, 'I have an appointment with God.' Then I would smile as I mentally marked off the days. I was so spiritual, a cut above all the rest. Why wouldn't God want to meet up with someone as eager as I was? I ask you!

Well, my friend dropped me off there with two ten-gallon plastic containers filled to the top with water. I didn't tell anyone where I was going or what I was planning to do except the friend who transported me. He was going to pick me up in ten days' time. I didn't waste any water bathing, and I took only two sets of clothes with me. I felt like John the Baptist but without a river or a shower nearby. From this point on, it all goes downhill fast.

When it came to timing, I had chosen poorly. A heatwave moved across the state that week, and I was baking like a potato (115° F/46° C). I couldn't escape the direct rays of the sun because there was nowhere to retreat, except my tent, which was like an oven. I should have brought some tea bags because the water was hot enough to brew them. Ten days later, when I returned to civilization, I was so sunburnt that the skin was peeling off me, and I was as thin as a starving grasshopper.

I read my Bible, but most of the time I was miserable, hungry, hot and bored. I had nowhere to go and nothing to do. John, at least, had people come to be baptized. All I had was grassland, an empty stomach, rattlesnakes, unrelenting sunshine and a distant bull to avoid.

You will be pleased to hear that God kept the appointment. My quest was not in vain. He arrived and spoke to me on the first morning before I brushed my teeth. It was annoying. I believe he said, 'Richard, I want you to shave your beard.'

Now, for those who are follically challenged or narcissistic chin exhibitionists, this wouldn't be a big deal, but those of us who sport a well-crafted beard down to our chest will understand my angst. Lay the sacrifice on the altar, and God sends the fire, but I didn't want to lay it down or cut it off. For ten gruelling days, I fought it. I just couldn't do it. I couldn't even pray. I'd hidden behind this beard for over fifteen years. It was my last vestige of hippie coolness – an idol hanging from my face.

I finally gave in and shaved the monster. Today I have a little chin stubble, but the idol is gone. When I eventually resettled myself in civilization, I came across this Bible verse; you may have read it.

> Does the Lord delight in burnt offerings and sacrifices
> > as much as in obeying the Lord?
> To obey is better than sacrifice,
> > and to heed is better than the fat of rams.
>
> *(1 Sam. 15:22)*

I went out into the desert to meet with God, but my idyllic aspirations bit the dust before the first hunger pang of the fast. I went out hoping for visions of God like those of Ezekiel[3] or holy encounters like Isaiah's vivid experience in the temple.[4] Instead, God branded a lesson on my heart that I will never forget: 'To obey is better than sacrifice.' Our offerings mean nothing if we don't come wanting to hear and willing to obey. Obedience is God's love language, the language of adoration.[5] Jesus was adamant about this: 'If you love me, keep my commands.'[6]

When God asks us to do something, it's not at our choice of time; it's not our idea or always for our benefit, but for his. The reward for obedience is a profounder relationship with Jesus. Obedience is how we honour and worship God. Obedience draws us closer to him, and the closer we get to him, the more we love him. Our priorities become fine-tuned to the will of heaven.

Obedience is to love Jesus more than the mission, more than our prayers, more than worship, more than learning the word, more than our entertainment, and more than our expectations. Obedience is how we show our love for God without agenda or benefit. We just want to please him and live in his presence and favour.

When God speaks and reveals himself through the Holy Spirit, we don't keep him waiting. We worship and leave everything else undone. We drop everything and obey. He becomes the most important concern of each moment of each day – as he said, 'Abide in me'. This is how we keep the oil in our lamps and the fire burning.

Obedience is often awkward and uncomfortable. We immediately wonder how our obedience will affect those around us. How will Zoe react to my resignation from the board? How will they get along without me? How will it affect my wife and family if I obey God and move to another town? The questions are endless. They are born out of the wisdom of this world, but the voice of heaven knows what's best in all situations. God is working from an eternal perspective. His agenda goes beyond our understanding. The best thing for us to do is to co-operate, step out, trust and obey.

A wise friend once told me, 'The best thing you can do for everybody around you is to obey God.' I believe that is true. If God is asking me to quit my job, then the best thing I can do for my family and my boss is to quit. This is the life of a servant; this is the life of an ambassador. It's not religion; it's based on a living, interactive relationship with God.

One of the most frustrating things about obedience, though, is when God tells us to wait. No one likes to wait. Have you ever cursed your computer, ready to toss it out of the window because it takes three minutes to log on? If so, then you know what I'm talking about. Waiting isn't built into our fallen DNA.

God's guidance is perfect; it's not bound by space and time. God has a different modus operandi. His agenda is to prepare us for the new heavens and the new earth. He's moulding us for life everlasting, not just for the here and now. He wants to build into us a legacy that speaks beyond our years of service. When God tells us to wait, eternity is the goal – trust and obey.

Jesus sacrificed himself for us, but the timing of his death was crucial. Have you ever wondered why God didn't allow Jesus to be killed by Herod? Why wait until he was in his thirties? Why not send the perfect holy lamb to the slaughter when he was two years old? People were already being introduced to him and knew who he was; there were Mary and Joseph, the shepherds, the Magi, Simeon, and Anna in the temple.

I have also wondered about God's reluctance to execute Jesus in Nazareth. Why hold back when the citizens tried to throw him over a cliff? Wouldn't that be a picture of the scapegoat who took the sins of the nation out of the camp?[7] Why wait? The disciples and many of the people were beginning to follow him and talk about him.[8] Wasn't this enough to fulfil and continue the mission?

The primary reason wasn't the means of execution; it had everything to do with the quality of the sacrifice. In his humanity, Jesus learned the cost of obedience.[9] In his humanity, he experienced what it is like to resist sin.[10] He had to grow in wisdom as a human being.[11]

The sacrifice of Jesus took place when the offering was perfected – not that he wasn't perfect as God, but the humanity he took upon himself as the second Adam was being perfected, or perhaps a better word is 'completed'. This had to take place in space and time, but the goal was for eternity. The quality of the sacrifice was honed through obedience. It bequeathed a legacy that changed the course of history, the fate of creation and the salvation of humanity.

I am learning that when God says 'go', don't delay – go. I am also learning that when he instructs me to slow down and stop, I wait. I halt until he instructs me to proceed. This will bring glory to God and remind us that we are not of this world; we are on the path to eternity, and our instructions come from above, not from space and time. Our guidance is not bound to an earthly calendar or timepiece. Rushing ahead may have some positive outcomes on our planet, but not in heaven.

When Jesus saw the commitment and obedience of his disciples, he told them, 'I no longer call you servants . . . I have called you friends.'[12] That is the reward for obedience to the voice of God.

> Lord, help me to move beyond biblical speculation, hoping to source, 'What Would Jesus Do? (WWJD)' By your Holy Spirit, open my eyes and ears to know, 'What is Jesus calling me to do right now?' May I be a doer of love and not just one of its proclaimers.

The computer has become the primary information centre in every home. Sometimes my computer needs a reboot. Sometimes the programmes I use need an upgrade. Many upgrades are to protect my system from evil programmers and nefarious scams that try to rob me. I wish I could upgrade my brain as easily as I upgrade my system. It seems God has left that part up to us, and it is imperative that we are constantly on it, adjusting the way we think.[1]

The Bible counsels us to renew our minds,[2] upgrade them, and, at times, reboot the system. We are to fill our heads with noble thoughts[3] and keep our focus on the things above, such as God's word and his kingdom.[4] It's not an easy task, but the discipline is critical for our future wellbeing. As Solomon, the wisest man on earth, once said: 'Above all else, guard your heart, for everything you do flows from it.'[5]

It's our mind that guards our hearts. Our mind is the sentinel, the cherubim with the flaming sword. Think of it like this: We are standing in the middle of a room. It has one door. We hold the key; no one else can touch, copy or hold it. We are the guards. We are powerful, and nothing will enter our room unless we give it permission. I hear a knock on the door.

'Who is it?'

'It's me. I have the words of Jesus to share with you.'

'Great, come on in and instruct me.'

Then we hear another knock on the door. It sounds urgent and doesn't let up – bang, bang, bang. We go there.

'Who is this?'

'It's me.'

'Who is me?'

It's me, I'm Mr Lust. Let me in. I brought some films I want to show you. Images guaranteed to excite and entertain – ooh la la!

This is where we make a choice. Am I going to welcome him into my mind or am I going to slam the door in his evil face? I am the protector and guardian of my heart. If I hesitate, I have already lost because he knows how to slip in around me. I let the guard down on my heart the moment I gave way.

'Oh, come in, Mr Lust. Welcome. Sit down here and amuse me for a while. No one else will notice or know you were ever here.'

Thus begins the deception. It's scary. Mr Lust now has an open door to my heart, and he will take advantage of it. We begin to recognize his knock, and the more times we open the door to him, the tighter the grip on our hearts becomes. Eventually, it's an open-door policy, and the sin we thought we could control now controls us. Mr Lust is no longer a visitor but has taken up residence. It's much easier to slam the door than it is to expel someone who has moved in and rearranged the furniture.

King David did well until he started ogling Bathsheba. It changed the course of his life. King Saul didn't guard his heart either, and it cost him the throne. Judas was the same, he started doing little things like stealing money from the pockets of Jesus and the disciples.[6] It led him to the ultimate betrayal, all because he didn't guard his heart and the thoughts that influenced it. Obviously, his inner cognitions weren't that righteous or noble.

Conversely, Job was a man who protected his inner life. His righteousness was so well-established that God singled him out from the crowd and allowed Satan to test him. However, the test was more for the benefit of Satan and the angels of heaven than it was for Job. Job stood the test because of his determination to guard his heart from the thoughts that corrupt it.

> I made a covenant with my eyes
>> not to look lustfully at a young woman.
>
> *(Job 31:1)*

However, we don't renew our minds just by going around slamming doors – there is more to it. Many times, we need to reboot the system and apply the upgrades. We replace an old thought or idea with a new, improved one. We open the door and welcome what is pure, righteous and holy. We change the way we think. We learn from the Bible and godly teachers and engage in the right kind of conversation. 'Do not be misled: "Bad company corrupts good character."'[7]

If you feel down, I would ask you, 'What have you been thinking about?' Are we filling our minds and hearts with the thoughts of God or the thoughts of this world? Are we listening to what people think of us or to what God thinks and says about us? Do we keep rehearsing all the mistakes and sins of the past, or are we thanking God for his grace, forgiveness and mercy at the present moment? Are we filling our minds with God's word or television? It matters. We stand guard. Our thoughts steer our hearts, and they influence everything we do and say. It's difficult to be awesome if we don't upgrade our thinking and protect our hearts from the pollution and evil that wants to deceive and kill us off. Let's renew our minds and be awesome every day. I don't think there would be any objection from God if we sang this simple little children's song to ourselves now and then, 'Oh be Careful, Little Eyes, What You See.'

40

Laugh

Nehemiah tells us that the joy of the Lord is our strength.[1] Jesus told us his joy would be in us and fill us completely.[2] In the book of Hebrews, we are told that Jesus had more joy than any other living person.[3] This is what sustained him throughout his ministry. There wasn't any joy on the cross, but Jesus bore it for 'the joy that was set before him.'[4] Even the very thought of joy strengthened him. You wonder why joy is usually the first quality we surrender when trouble comes.

In the Bible, the word 'joy' appears about 218 times, while the words 'happy' and 'happiness' occur around 26 times.[5] It seems God is more concerned about our joy than he is about our happiness, even though at times it's hard to differentiate between the two, but one thing is certain: joy is not swayed by circumstances because it is not of this world. It's a fruit of the Holy Spirit. The source is God, not winning the lottery or having a good time on the beach.

The fruit of the Holy Spirit lists nine specific qualities that God desires us to walk in. We tend to concentrate on the attributes relating to our behaviour:[6] be kind, good, faithful, and show a bit of love and self-control. We don't easily let them drop when we face the world, but we tend to hold joy lightly. Is joy any less of an attribute than kindness? Is joy hit-and-miss while faithfulness is constant?

I am grateful that joy doesn't depend on us to manufacture it or to wait for something good to trigger it. The Holy Spirit releases it in us through faith and abiding in Jesus. Of course, we will rejoice with those who rejoice and mourn with those who mourn,[7] but we can't let circumstances, the world or the devil rob us of that which sustained Jesus in his ministry or the people of Israel in the book of Nehemiah. Joy, like love and goodness, should be constant in our lives.

Paul speaks of joy sixteen times in the book of Philippians. It's considered the most joyful book of the Bible. What speaks even louder is that he wrote this letter from prison. It's hard to live in joy if we complain about our lot and the seemingly unfair circumstances that overtake us. We could toss more logs on the fire of worry, but it will never keep us warm or put a smile on our face. This joy that Paul and the Bible speak about is not of this world. It comes from the Holy Spirit inside of us. It's as vital to a Spirit-filled life as love, peace, kindness and goodness.

Yeah, but do I have a right to be joyful with all the suffering I see in the world around me? Yes, it's not only a right; it is necessary, and it is of God. It is our strength. We are not of this world. This godly joy is contagious and attractive. This kind of joy is what the world is looking for but can only find when things go in their favour. They have no say when joy or happiness will creep up on them, and it easily slips away when things go dark. Not so, with the joy of the Lord. We can't let the world, the six o'clock news, politics, or negative people rob us of this gift from God.

> Further, my brothers and sisters, rejoice in the Lord! It is no trouble for me to write the same things to you again, and it is a safeguard for you.
>
> *(Phil 3:1)*

> Rejoice in the Lord always. I will say it again: rejoice!
>
> *(Phil. 4:4)*

It's a spiritual discipline to rejoice in the Lord. It's a choice we make in all circumstances. But why should we rejoice in the Lord always, in all circumstances? We do it because it opens up our hearts to walk in and let loose the joy of heaven. Rejoice in the Lord, and you won't be worrying about what is going on around you, you will be a source of strength, a ray of hope and sunshine.

Grumpiness is not an attribute of God or a fruit of the Holy Spirit. Who wants to become a Christian when they see us complaining and just as down and entangled with the cares of this world as everyone else? I remember looking at some old photos of past Christian conventions. You know, those long black-and-white panoramas with a few hundred people standing on the steps of a church building? Maybe it was a cultural thing but, as I looked at all their faces, only about two of them were smiling. I don't know about you, but I thought, 'Who wants to join that club?' Is the holy life a sombre, grumpy life? No way! God is not grumpy, and we are called to be like him, not like the world.

Look at what happened to Paul and Silas after they delivered a girl from a spirit of divination.[8] They were marched before the city magistrates, accused of sedition against Rome. They were stripped naked.[9] Then they were beaten with rods (the officials would carry bundles of rods with them for such occasions). This was serious. After which, they were thrown into a windowless prison and chained to a wall by their feet. That would make most of us grumpy. I could understand the lack of smiles if we had that photo. However, Paul practised what he preached, and the adventure was truly awesome.

> About midnight Paul and Silas were praying and singing hymns to God, and the other prisoners were listening to them.
>
> *(Acts 16:25)*

They were rejoicing in the Lord. Then God sent an earthquake, and the prisoners were free to run, but Paul stayed, told the jailer about Jesus, and ended up in the jailer's house, baptizing his entire family. It's an awesome life. The ambassador of the kingdom of God draws from the wells of heaven, not this earth, so why shouldn't we rejoice and be filled with the joy of the Lord? In his presence is joy. Put him on.

> You make known to me the path of life;
>> you will fill me with joy in your presence,
>> with eternal pleasures at your right hand.
>
> *(Ps. 16:11)*

If you think Paul is radical, then listen to James. He takes it to another level: 'Consider it pure joy, my brothers and sisters, whenever you face trials of many kinds.'[10] We often give this lip service, but how often do we put it into practice? It's a wild way to look at life. It's otherworldly and a little crazy, but we're not of this world. Joy gives us strength to run the race and fulfil the mission. Circumstances can't smother the joy from above. It gives us a heavenly perspective. Let's embrace our kingdom passport and receive from God.

> For the kingdom of God is not a matter of eating and drinking, but of righteousness, peace and joy in the Holy Spirit.
>
> *(Rom. 14:17)*

My wife often hears me laughing to myself – not maniacally, just chuckling under my breath. So she asks me what's so amusing. I honestly tell her, 'I'm not laughing about anything. I just sense a joy in my heart.' I find this can be a daily experience in all circumstances – even in the midst of great loss. As Paul also tells us, 'Brothers and sisters, we do not want you to be uninformed about those who sleep in death, so that you do not grieve like the rest of mankind, who have no hope.'[11]

Consider the hymn written by the prophet Habakkuk. Babylon was beating down the door of the nation. Life was grim because Babylon had a scorched-earth policy; they would destroy everything useful to the enemy: towns, fields, orchards and other food supplies. Yet here is what Habakkuk and the faithful would be singing in the temple.

> Though the fig-tree does not bud
>   and there are no grapes on the vines,
> though the olive crop fails
>   and the fields produce no food,
> though there are no sheep in the sheepfold
>   and no cattle in the stalls,
> yet I will rejoice in the LORD,
>   I will be joyful in God my Saviour.
>
> The Sovereign LORD is my strength;
>   he makes my feet like the feet of a deer,
>   he enables me to tread on the heights.

(Hab. 3:17–19)

Now some of us may be thinking, 'Then why am I so down?' 'Why am I so sad?' 'Why don't I sense the joy of the Lord in my life?' I explain it like this: Imagine an aeroplane full of joy orbiting the runway of your heart. The jet flew in from heaven and has your name on it. The pilot circles the runway and radios up to the command centre, saying, 'I want to land but I can't see the landing strip. It's too cloudy down there. There is unconfessed sin, and there sure is a lot of complaining, worry and selfish talk about all the negativities of life, the world and their circumstances. There just isn't enough expectation, hope, faith or thankfulness to light the runway for a landing.'

God doesn't hold back, but at times we allow things to creep into our lives that can obscure the landing strip. God just instructs the pilot to keep circling: 'I forecast the weather. One day the clouds will part, then you will land the plane.'

King David lost his joy in the Bathsheba affair, but he didn't give up on the goodness of God. His prayer of repentance often finds itself in our Christian worship. It's interesting that the one thing David missed the most was the joy of the Lord! It is our strength.

> Create in me a pure heart, O God,
>   and renew a steadfast spirit within me.
> Do not cast me from your presence
>   or take your Holy Spirit from me.
> Restore to me the joy of your salvation
>   and grant me a willing spirit, to sustain me.
>
> *(Ps. 51:10–12)*

If you are just having a bad day, as a small exercise, I would tell you to say the name Jesus. Think of him and smile as you say it. At times, I find this practice helpful to prime the pump and release the joy that comes from heaven – it's out of this world. Don't take yourself so seriously, and don't forget to laugh – especially at yourself. We can all be jerks at one time or another. Lighten up, your concerns are not the centre of the universe. 'The sky is clear, Lord; land the plane.' Yee-haw!

41

Give

The Emerald Isle (where I live) isn't just the land of saints and scholars or the elusive leprechaun. The Celtic use of the English language also has its fair share of mystery and intrigue. I can't count how many times I've scratched my head trying to understand my Irish wife. We've been married for a number of decades, and she still lobs new idioms at me – words she never spoke before. Here are a few she's voiced over the years.

'You're an eejit.'

'You're not the full shilling.'

'You're a chancer.'

'You're acting the maggot.'

'You have the face of a Lurgan spade.'

Ah, the bliss. I think she's just searching for a better way to call me 'sweetheart'. Someday we'll both smile and know what she's talking about.

Every culture loves to stir the language pot and pull out new idioms and turns of phrase. We just can't help ourselves. The ancient culture of the Bible also had its fair share of idioms. The point is that if we don't recognize these expressions, we will try to interpret them literally and fall down a rabbit hole. If a future time-traveller read some of the messages I receive on social media, they would be in trouble: 'It's raining cats and dogs here at the moment, and to make matters worse, my neighbour has a hole in their head and keeps spouting rubbish.'

If we weren't familiar with these idioms, we would try to interpret them literally. That's the rabbit hole I'm talking about, it clouds the issue. Jesus often employed idioms to convey his message. If we don't recognize them, we won't understand what he's really saying. Consider these well-worn words from the Sermon on the Mount.

> The lamp of the body is the eye. If therefore your eye is good, your whole body will be full of light. But if your eye is bad, your whole body will be full of darkness. If therefore the light that is in you is darkness, how great *is* that darkness!
>
> *(Matt. 6:22–3, NKJV)*

How many times have you heard a sermon based on these few sentences? Speakers usually go down the path of devotion. 'If you keep your eyes on Jesus, you will be all right, but if your sight is bad and you focus on the world, you will be in darkness.' These statements are true but, in this instance, that's not what Jesus is talking about.

Jesus is employing two Jewish idioms here that have been floating around in Jewish culture since the time of Moses: the 'good eye' and the 'evil eye'.[1] The meaning would be clear to listeners of his day, but not so clear to us. A person with an evil eye is miserly and stingy with what they have. A person with a good eye is generous with their money, time and possessions. This is what Jesus is saying. He's talking about our attitude and behaviour when it comes to money and what we receive, own and possess – the assets people run after in this world. The giver is full of light; the miser is full of darkness.

I find it helpful to compare these words to a dying star. Scientists tell us that when a massive star reaches the end of its evolutionary stage, it either explodes or collapses in on itself. One is called a supernova; the other is a black hole.

Supernovas explode outward, throwing light across its solar system and beyond. The black hole, scientists tell us, forms when a giant star implodes. The gravitational pull is so strong that everything is sucked into it. Light can't even escape its force. That's why it's called a 'black hole'. It's not that the essence of light is non-existent in a black hole; it just can't shine or escape. To our eyes, darkness dominates.

Metaphorically, we could say that the supernova is generous and the black hole is miserly. The supernova is spewing outward, giving abundant light to everything surrounding it. The black hole is hoarding everything and pulling it into itself, even the light. This is what I believe Jesus is communicating when he says, 'If therefore the light that is in you is darkness, how great is that darkness!' This is not a compliment.

The context of this passage deals primarily with what we do with money and possessions. Listen to the Jewish translation of this verse. It interprets the idiom for us.

> For where your wealth is, there your heart will be also. 'The eye is the lamp of the body.' So if you have a 'good eye' [that is, if you are generous] your whole body will be full of light; but if you have an 'evil eye' [if you are stingy] your whole body will be full of darkness. If, then, the light in you is darkness, how great is that darkness! No one can be slave to two masters; for he will either hate the first and love the second, or scorn the second and be loyal to the first. You can't be a slave to both God and money.
> (Matt. 6:21–4, CJB)

I talk a lot in this book about God's provision. I don't believe he gave because I earned it or was worthy of it, but I do believe he knows my heart. By his grace, I am a giver and not a miser. I am not going to let my left hand know what my right hand is doing,[2] but I will say that what I receive I freely give.

Richard, do you believe in tithing? I would say 'yes' and 'no'. I believe we should give everything. We are to be supernovas in our community, spreading light. I don't think about percentages of what I should contribute, whether in the Christian community or outside of it. If the thought of proportions enters my head at all, it focuses more on what I am choosing to keep. I believe Jesus when he says we should be laying up our treasures in heaven's bank, and not the banks of earth.[3] As John Wesley purportedly said, 'It's not how much of my money will I give to God, but how much of God's money will I keep for myself.'

St Francis of Assisi has always inspired me. He owned nothing, and what he acquired he gave to those in need. He would walk into town fully clothed but return home naked because he had given his clothes to the poor. Radical? Yes. Otherworldly? I believe so. There are many radical givers in this world and throughout our history. The really great givers are the ones we never hear about because they do it in secret. If we do hear about their giving, it's not because they blew their own trumpet; it's just that the paparazzi of their day broadcast it. Consider the New Testament story of the widow's mite.[4]

One Sunday morning, I was sitting in the hippie church I attended. The collection platter came around, but giving money that day just wasn't enough. So I took out my wallet and threw the whole thing onto the plate: my driver's licence, photos, money, and cards – everything that related to my life, my legal identity and my privileges. I laughed all the way home, singing, 'I surrender all, I surrender all; all to thee, my blessed Saviour, I surrender all.'

I felt like I stepped out of the boat that day. In the world's eyes, that was crazy. I agree, but in heaven's eyes, I surrendered all! Giving is not about the money; it's about the heart. One thing is certain: if God has your heart, he also has your purse, your wallet, your time, your devotion, your obedience and your life.

A couple of years later, my pastor handed the wallet back to me. He didn't say a word. He had a lot to deal with in a church full of young radicals. God bless him. However, we weren't suffering from LSD flashbacks; we were acutely aware we were no longer of this world, but God so loved the world that he gave. We knew it, and we wanted to please him and be like him.

No one gets a warm, gushy feeling when they encounter a miser. The light of Jesus isn't shining through them, but the supernovas of this world are awesome. I hope to be one of them. By God's grace, I pray that the treasures I have accumulated in heaven will far outweigh anything I have hoarded on earth. This stirs the adventure, and I want to jump into the depths of that stirring – not wade about in a splash pool counting how much I can afford or whether I can manage 10 per cent.

42

Serve

It's funny the dreams we have when we are ill. One morning, as I was grievously floundering in virus mode, I told my wife I had just had a nightmare. She said she heard me cry out in my sleep. I dreamed that ten people were sitting in the kitchen. I didn't invite them; they just showed up. I felt like Bilbo Baggins when all these uninvited folk arrived at his house and ate all his grub.[1] Well, not wanting to be rude, I asked them if they would like a cup of tea – this is what you do in Northern Ireland. The nightmare began when they all said 'yes' – ten cups of tea. My immediate response was, 'Noooooo!'

I woke up shaking – traumatized. My wife then questioned the validity of my dream evaluation: 'That's not a nightmare!' she told me.

I really didn't want to discuss if my dream was bona fide or not, so I coughed, wiped my nose, and went back to sleep. To me, that was a nightmare. Who wants to serve tea when they are suffering on the bed of affliction? I ask you.

The landed gentry and the aristocracy of Britain's past usually had their fair share of servants attending the house and serving tea. Many are attracted to that world: *Downton Abbey*, Jane Austen and *The Crown*. We like to be served, and a bit of pampering never goes amiss. Power and control are also big draws for people. James and John, the sons of thunder, vied for hierarchical positions and displays of power. Jesus was always steering them towards a more kingdom-of-God approach and attitude.

Then James and John, the sons of Zebedee, came to him. 'Teacher,' they said, 'we want you to do for us whatever we ask.'

'What do you want me to do for you?' he asked.

They replied, 'Let one of us sit at your right and the other at your left in your glory.'

(Mark 10:35–7)

James and John were asking this when the other disciples weren't around – for obvious reasons. 'When the ten heard about this, they became indignant.'[2] Why? probably because the other ten disciples didn't think of asking it first.[3] The Thunder Boys offended them, but here's how Jesus guides the conversation.

You know that those who are regarded as rulers of the Gentiles lord it over them, and their high officials exercise authority over them. Not so with you. Instead, whoever wants to become great among you must be your servant, and whoever wants to be first must be slave of all. For even the Son of Man did not come to be served, but to serve, and to give his life as a ransom for many.

(Mark 10:42–5)

Jesus doesn't quash their hubris or spiritual ambition; he steers it.[4] You can be great, even awesome, but the path to get there isn't promoted or laid out the way the world has obviously taught and influenced you. To go up, you have to bend down. To rule, you have to serve. To lead, you have to humbly follow. Everyone in the kingdom of God is a servant, because that's the way the King of the kingdom chooses to live.

The cure for pride is not to put on a mask of humility. If you want to grow in humility, then serve. The cure for pride is service. I can't help but be impressed and inspired by former

US President, Jimmy Carter. After he leaves the White House, he links up with Habitat for Humanity, a non-profit worldwide organization offering decent housing for the homeless to live in. He stands on ladders, paints people's hallways, and pounds nails, providing and improving homes. He is rich and could live a life like Solomon, but he humbly chooses to serve and advocate for the homeless. I think God smiles at that. Who is the greatest among us, the President of the United States or the person holding a paintbrush and a hammer for the sake of others?[5] I think the Thunder Boys could learn a lesson or two from this former dignitary, but couldn't we all?

> Now that I, your Lord and Teacher, have washed your feet, you also should wash one another's feet. I have set you an example that you should do as I have done for you.
>
> *(John 13:14–15)*

Here's a parable that often challenges my 'dream' reluctance to serve tea.[6] It's not found in the Bible, but it's scripturally motivated.

Joe Schwartz was hired by KofG[7] Enterprises. He didn't have an office or a room with a window to look out of; instead, he was given a mop, a kettle and a closet full of cleaning supplies. His room was located in the basement. If someone called him for a cup of tea, Joe would serve it. If an office needed cleaning, Joe was the man. He was the nameless tidy-king, the broom handler – the detergent dude with an on-call kettle to make and serve the tea and coffee.

Joe soon learned the building was organized by role and importance. The CEO was on the top floor. The vice president was on the floor below him, and the other floors housed the sales clerks and the administration staff.

For a while, Joe was content being on-call, making tea and coffee, and cleaning up the joint. He served them well. Then one day he was thinking about the administration clerks in the office above him. They were invited to office parties and received more kudos and money from the firm, so he makes a wish. 'I sure would like to be one of the admin people sitting in the office above me.' Immediately, his aspiration was granted.

He enjoyed his new position until he began to think about the people on the higher floor. They didn't have to share an office. They each had one of their own. They were more important; they were the sales clerks. So Joe made another wish. 'I want to be like the sales clerks on the floor above me.' Straightaway, he secured his new position.

He was getting the hang of this wishing thing. 'I want to be the vice president.' Again, he was transported to the upper storey. There, his name was embossed on the door: Vice President Joe Schwartz. Promotion led to entitlement, and entitlement led to promotion. So, why not shoot for the top? 'I wish I was the CEO, the president of the company, being served on the highest level of the building.' Splash! There he was, the big fish in a little pond.

Life was sweet until he stepped out onto the roof and looked up. The cogs of ambition were grinding away in his head. God is up there somewhere above me. So why not make one more wish? 'I wish I was like God.' Then came the flash of lightning, and there was Joe – back in the basement, sweeping the floor, dusting the furniture and serving tea – awesome.

The greatest among you will be your servant. For those who exalt themselves will be humbled, and those who humble themselves will be exalted.

(Matt. 23:11–12)

Do nothing out of selfish ambition or vain conceit. Rather, in humility value others above yourselves, not looking to your own interests but each of you to the interests of the others.

(Phil. 2:3–4)

If you can relate to this, then let's make this our prayer: 'Father, I know I will never be Lord. I know I will never be king. I know I will never be a celebrity. I know I am not a major voice or recognized force in this world, but please guide and help me to be one of the best, unnamed, unknown servants in this generation, and grant me the grace to rejoice and laugh with you at the very thought of it. Amen.'

'Would you like a cup of tea?'

43

Restore

I had a wart. Like a big mushroom planted on my thumb, it was aggressive and alive. I had unwillingly hosted the beast for over twenty years. Periodically, I'd chop off its head with the nail clippers, but it stood its ground and continued to grow. I walked it to the medical centre, hoping it wouldn't resist or challenge the genius of modern science. I watched as the doctor assaulted it with liquid nitrogen. The monster whimpered, but days later it laughingly lifted its belligerent head, mocking all my attempts to put it down.

So one morning, as I was reading and praying, I was drawn to my unwanted tenant. My thought was, 'You have no right to be here, but how should I pray?' Then I started to examine my faith and belief in divine healing. In the Bible and church practice, I see two primary models at work. When Jesus and the disciples prayed for healing, it was immediate. They had the power and the gift to heal.[1] The first model of healing has to do with the gift. It's an instantaneous miracle executed by God through an individual.

Of all the miracles performed in the New Testament, it was the gift of healing that opened people to the glory and love of God. Not many knew about the 'water into wine' incident. Most of the participants eating the miraculous loaves and fish didn't jump around rejoicing in the miracle; even the disciples missed a beat on that one. But when a leper was cleansed, a lame person got up and started to walk, or the demonised were freed and healed, people stood in awe.[2] Their eternal-microchip-beeper started to smoke and burn in them because the gift of healing informs the heart more than the mind. It's emotive. We love to see lost potential rise up with new hope and possibilities, and we also love to witness freedom from death and pain – a restoration of what was lost and robbed.

The second model isn't as dramatic, but it's no less awesome. It's more of a community affair. The results aren't often instantaneous, but there is still a restorative recovery.

> Is anyone among you sick? Let them call the *elders* [plural] of the *church* to pray over them and anoint them with oil in the name of the Lord. And the prayer offered in faith will make the sick person well; the Lord will raise them up.
>
> *(Jas 5:14–15, italics mine)*

Not everyone has the gift to heal, but the community of faith has been given the divine right to participate in the healing process. In the second model, the person's restoration is often progressive. This is no less a miracle than the gift of healing; it's just not as sensational. This doesn't mean I have to be physically present in a quorum of Christians, but I know others in the church are also praying to the same end – restoration, health and freedom from pain.

Now we can't make these two healing models into laws because there are many adaptations. For example, Jesus had the power of the gift, but he never followed the same pattern or used the same prayer. He would spit on the ground and rub mud in a blind man's eye;[3] the community of faith is instructed to administer oil. Muddy spittle just wouldn't go down well in the church today. Jesus would speak a command, even from a great distance, and see positive results.[4] Peter would make a declaration and then grab a lame man's hand to help him up.[5] Other times, his shadow (or close proximity) healed people.[6] Paul's handkerchief laid on the sick brought recovery.[7]

However, every model of healing requires the leading of the Holy Spirit. When we leave the Spirit's guidance out of the equation, we don't often see that many recoveries. He's in charge of the miracle, not us. We don't know how to pray as we should – one prayer doesn't fit all.

So back to my uninvited guest. That morning, after the above thoughts and discussion had whirled about in my head, I declared war on the wart. I stood my ground with the shield of faith and prayed.

> Lord, I don't have enough faith to believe this wart will instantly fall off my thumb onto my lap, but I do believe that, from this moment on, it's going to progressively shrink and die. I have faith that it will be completely gone in one month.

After that prayer, I stared at the thing. Then I lifted the sword of the Spirit and struck the defining blow.

> I curse you, wart, in the name of Jesus Christ, and I command you to start shrinking from this day forward, and in thirty days you'll be gone. Amen.

By the thirty-first day, my thumb was freed from the wart's tyranny. It had died and bitten the dust. The beast was con-quered. I was amazed, or should I say, 'awed'? It was actually gone! God is so good. He's always teaching us and opening our eyes and ears to the movement of his Spirit. He wants us to know his ways, not just his deeds. So I told the wart story to a Christian friend. A few months later, he too had a wart story to share.

Richard, I was fascinated by your wart tale. When I went home that day, I was thinking about a wart I had. It had been with me for years, so I followed your example. I also didn't have the faith that it would instantly disappear, but I could stretch my faith to thirty days. So that's how I prayed and cursed the thing. Thirty days later, it too was gone.

Wow! That was an awesome surprise. God is on the move; we just need to learn how to keep in step with him – experiment, gamble, step out, learn his ways and then walk in them. He wants us to grow and be Jesus in this world.

Now, surprisingly, this isn't the end of the story. A couple of years ago, I was the guest speaker at a church and told them, 'The Tale of Two Warts'. I said, 'I think God has given me the gift of wart eradication.' People laughed but, at the end of the sermon, a man came up and showed me his wart and asked me to pray the 'eradicating prayer'. I know I'm not to make this into a formula, but I prayed the way my friend and I had addressed our own wart extermination.

Months later, I met with the pastor of that church, who had been absent the day I visited his congregation. I told him the wart stories, because that's what I do; tell out the glories of God. Then, to my surprise, he said, 'So that's what it was all about. Sam at the church told me about someone praying for his wart, and it is now gone. I thought that was strange at the time, but now I know the whole story.'

Moving forward, I was teaching a class at the Nazarene Theological College in Manchester, England. The morning of the first class, I woke up with all the signs of the flu. I remember standing there, looking in the mirror, and saying to myself, 'This isn't right. I spent weeks preparing to teach this course, and the students have come to learn. I can't arrive with the flu on the first morning.' So I prayed, 'Lord, I don't believe these symptoms will leave my body immediately, but I believe if I give you time to work, you will heal me.' As I looked in the mirror, I announced before God and myself, 'I do not accept these germs or these symptoms, and I command you in the name of Jesus to be completely gone from my body within the next two hours before the students arrive.' That morning, I entered the classroom restored. The runny nose and sore throat were gone. That was one of the most enjoyable weeks I had teaching there.

In all situations, the adventure-driven life is an ongoing, interactive and learning experience with God. Prayer and obedience to God's voice and leading are the interactions. If we only read the Bible and neglect communicating with our heavenly Father, we will fill our closets with masks and never grow into the robes God has provided and clothed us with. This will harden our hearts and keep us reaching for those Spirit-numbing umbrellas.

To be honest, I used to be conflicted about healing. For a season, I didn't want to be around sick people because I felt it was my Christian obligation to lay hands on them and pray for their recovery, but often their condition remained the same. Like most people, I find it frustrating to pray and not see the miracle or the hand of God at work. Some will say I lacked faith. Others will be thinking, 'Of course there was no healing; miracles ceased with the apostles.' I'm sure the court could present a long list of 'why nots' in this situation. Believe me, I wrestle with my own list, but I can't give up. I believe God wants to heal today with the same compassion and love with which Jesus healed on the streets of Jerusalem.

I'm also learning that the challenge to be God's conduit of blessing and power doesn't always require success, especially when it comes to those in poor health. My prayers should stem from the love of God in my heart, and that love should be evident whether the deaf hear or not. Yes, we want to walk in the power to heal. We may not see the miracle each time we pray, but we should always witness the love. Our call to be awesome should lap against the shores of heaven more than the shores of our community.

> Enoch walked faithfully with God; then he was no more, because God took him away.
>
> *(Gen. 5:24)*

> Have you considered my servant Job? There is no one on earth like him; he is blameless and upright, a man who fears God and shuns evil.
>
> *(Job 1:8)*

> And a voice from heaven said, 'This is my Son, whom I love; with him I am well pleased.'
>
> *(Matt. 3:17)*

Whatever model or mode God chooses to heal, whether we spit on the ground or pour the oil, we have to move beyond our formulas and be led by the Holy Spirit. Our success isn't measured by positive results, but by the love of God in our hearts and our willingness to listen and then step out and obey. Jesus wanted to heal the people of Nazareth, but their hard hearts limited what he desired to accomplish.

> He could not do any miracles there, except lay his hands on a few people who were ill and heal them. He was amazed at their lack of faith.
>
> *(Mark 6:5–6)*

The thing to consider in this verse is not the town's scepticism but the willingness of God to bless the people in miraculous ways. However, their unbelief constrained him. In the world's eyes, this probably wasn't one of his most successful days, but in the eyes of God, Jesus listened and obeyed, and that is what heaven values.

Not every wart disappears. Not every person prayed for gets out of bed, but the more I pray, the more I will see people healed. The more a church congregation prays in faith for the sick, the more positive results we will see. Here in the West, we think, 'Yes, God heals, but it was really the medicine and the doctors.' Of course, God gave us medicine and doctors to help the process along, and we are grateful, but I often say to people, 'You can never go wrong giving God the credit.'

As Solomon explained in Ecclesiastes, there is a season for all things – a time to be born and a time to die. The Holy Spirit teaches us how to pray. He knows the times and the seasons. Yes, we will pray for the pain to go away, but at times we need to be sensitive enough to let the person go. Hopefully, they will go to God in heaven, and we will pray their final steps will be restful and pain-free. Remember, home is just one last breath away, and that too can be awesome.

When I returned home from the Vietnam War, I went off-grid. I purchased two acres of land in Kansas, hiding out in the middle of nowhere in a tepee. The acreage was full of brambles and trees. If you didn't follow the overgrown, winding path, you would probably do yourself damage. Back then, I wasn't a Christian following Jesus. I guess you could say I was working for the dark side – the other guy.

One day, one of my Vietnam buddies came by for a visit. We sat around the fire that was burning in the middle of the tepee. We smoked the peace pipe and drank a few bottles of wine. We were drunk, ripped, spaced-out, and hippie-fied, flying high and crashing like the blimp pictured on the first Led Zeppelin album.

Unfortunately for my friend, there were no street lights outside the door, and cloud cover extinguished the night sky. Beyond the exit was a 'black hole', and I didn't have a torch or flashlight to lend him. Around midnight, my friend got up and wanted to drive home, but he had to get to his car. My servant's heart wasn't activated back then, so when he asked me to lead him down the path to his car, I refused. Instead, I just told him to get out and start walking, and I would shout the directions at him. So he staggered out into the night. I hollered, 'Go straight ahead.' That's when he started cursing the brambles.

I continued to guide him. 'Now, turn right.' I heard the curses intensifying when he crashed into a tree. I continued

with my verbal map. 'Turn left.' 'Straight ahead, five steps.'
'Take a right.' He continued to curse and mumble as he was
whacked by trees, tripped by undergrowth, slapped by foliage,
and stabbed by various branches.

He finally gave up on my directions and drove off, spewing
gravel behind him. I hadn't had a clue how to guide him on
that path. I was just shouting out random directions, making
it up as I went along. The slapstick was thoroughly entertain-
ing, and the fuming expletives added to the comic panto-
mime. Aren't you glad Jesus saved me? I sure am!

This is what it's like when we listen to the wrong voice. We
end up in all kinds of hurtful situations, being steered and
laughed at by the gods of this world. We, as Christians, are
on a pilgrimage, walking a narrow path to glory, but we also
need some boundaries to keep us out of the brambles and not
smacking our heads against a tree. There are two verses I find
very helpful. They cover a lot of territory.

> Do not grieve the Holy Spirit of God.
>
> *(Eph. 4:30)*

> Do not quench the Spirit.
>
> *(1 Thess. 5:19)*

These are two spiritual billboards that mark the path, and we
need to respect them. They are the guidelines and the boundaries that illuminate the trail. One sits on the left side of the
road, the other on the right. We walk between them.

When we read these verses in context, we discover that
grieving the Spirit relates to the fruit and the character of God,
and quenching the Holy Spirit relates to the gifts.[1] Sometimes
Christians find themselves veering to one side of the road and

ignoring the other. Some denominations park their buses under the billboard, promoting spiritual gifts, while others hang
out on the opposite side of the road, emphasizing the fruit.

However, it's the same Spirit animating both the character
and the power of God. To say God is interested in one side of
the road more than the other is a personal, human doctrine
that compartmentalizes how God chooses to work in us and
on this planet. We need to navigate the divine middle, receiving from both sides, and not veer too far to the left or the
right. Why? Because this is the way Jesus walked, and we are
called to be like him.

Last year I was invited to a charismatic congregation to
speak on holiness. I loved their hunger. Then I received an
invitation from a conservative congregation to present a series
of seminars on the spiritual gifts.[2] I smiled and thanked God
for the open door and the opportunity to address both sides
of the road. It was an honour.

I know conservative congregations are wary of the gifts.
The gifts can be a messy business, and it's not easy for any
pastor or church team to steer. I find many are afraid because
of what they have seen and witnessed in hyper-charismania.
What I told the conservative congregation is that we usually
aren't offended by the gifts, but by the culture surrounding
them. Sometimes it's hard to draw a line between the two. I
invited the conservative congregation to look at it this way.

God is not calling any of us to adopt the social baggage that
often accompanies spiritual gifts. We don't have to receive the
gifts of the Spirit as potted plants, but let's be open to God and
receive them as divine seeds planted in our soil. What will they
look like as they grow and blossom in your denomination? Let

God fertilize them, not the culture you question and steer away from. Honour the gifts as seeds, gifts of love to be planted in your garden – the garden God has been cultivating throughout your history. He wants to progress it, not destroy it.

At the end of the seminars, I asked anyone who desired a particular gift to be activated in them to come forward and we would pray. To my surprise and delight, more than half of those attending came forward wanting to receive more from God. A few asked for the gift of tongues and interpretation; others desired one or more of the prophetic gifts, such as the word of knowledge, the word of wisdom, and prophecy. A few were drawn to the discerning of spirits. Others sought the gift of healing.

Obviously, we are all hungry for more – a deeper walk with God. Hunger awakens desire. We don't want to leave Jesus on the pages of a book. He's not a contractual, academic study guide handing out masks to promote his lifestyle and then giving us a divine boost into heaven. We long for his tangible presence. The yearning of the Holy Spirit compels us into the adventure. As St Patrick said: 'Christ with me, Christ before me, Christ behind me, Christ in me, Christ beneath me, Christ above me, Christ on my right, Christ on my left, Christ when I lie down, Christ when I sit down, and Christ when I arise.'[3]

Inwardly, our divine-microchip triggers a craving to work and walk with Jesus in a living, authentic, fully activated, tangible relationship. This is what glorifies God.

I was saved during the Jesus movement in the early seventies. The transition from hippie to saint was a wild ride of joy and expectation. We quickly learned that Jesus was steering his church toward a divine middle – a holy balance between love and power, gifts and fruit, faith and character.

This, to me, is biblical and is what Jesus considers to be the *normal* Christian life; it was never intended to be as controversial as we often make it. The gifts and the fruit go hand in hand. They are both from one God and one Spirit. When gifts are emphasized above the fruit of love and character, we miss the path and run into the brambles. When we emphasize the fruit of the Holy Spirit above the power gifts, our witness can become cerebral and academic.[4] If we want to be awesome, then we should steer toward the middle of the road. Why? Because that's where Jesus walks. As a matter of fact, he is the road!

When I pastored in Glasgow, I received a phone call from a friend. She said she was parked in a lot outside my apartment, and would I come down and talk to a young man who was sitting in the back seat of her car. He was an active user of heroin. I went. The moment I opened the back door and sat down next to him, he started cursing God at the top of his lungs. It was bizarre. He just kept looking up, spewing all these blasphemous words at the Almighty. That's not wise, and it certainly doesn't promote health. You could see the veins on his neck pumping blood to the brain. I believe it was a demonic manifestation.

My driver friend was a working mother with three young kids and was a bit flustered. I said to her, 'Let's praise God and declare his goodness.' We worshipped, sang and thanked God for all he was doing, while the young man screamed louder, descending into his own darkness. It was a strange encounter – we were using spiritual weapons, locked in hand-to-hand combat with an unseen, malevolent force.

This went on for about ten minutes, but we were now prepared for action. I turned to the young man, who was still in the middle of his ungodly rant, and commanded, 'In the name of Jesus, shut up!'

Immediately, the car was silent. It happened so quickly that my friend and I were amazed. The man relaxed in his seat and was in his right mind. We had just stepped into the book of Acts – come on in, the water's fine. We then had a lengthy discussion about Jesus. Three weeks later, he committed himself to the Lord and started attending an Elim congregation. God is so good.

What really floored me, though, was that the moment I opened the door to get out of the car he reached over and said, 'I just want to tell you that when I saw you coming towards me, a voice in my head kept shouting, "Run! Get away! Get out and run!"' Then the young man thanked me for seeing him. Now, that was awesome. Demons should be as afraid of us as they were of Jesus because we are his representatives in this world. God often directed his servants to be bold and cast off their fear.[1]

Put on Christ. We all must put on Christ. It's him in us – there is no power or spiritual influence in this world without him. We are ambassadors. We carry the treasure of the Holy Spirit in our mortal bodies. Have faith. Let Jesus live his life through you. We are Christ in this world. Let him do his thing – don't quench the Holy Spirit. We want to see his ministry, not our feeble, worldly attempts to promote him. We speak his word, but then we stand and let him reveal himself. This is the way all the apostles chose to live and minister.[2]

> 'Now, Lord, consider their threats and enable your servants to speak your word with great boldness. Stretch out your hand to heal and perform signs and wonders through the name of your holy servant Jesus.'
>
> After they prayed, the place where they were meeting was shaken. And they were all filled with the Holy Spirit and spoke the word of God boldly.
>
> *(Acts 4:29–31)*

These disciples were asking to be equipped beyond the capacity of human nature. Willingness is the open door for the filling power of the Spirit and the boldness to declare the name of Jesus. These followers learned from experience that standing strong is just as effective and powerful as kicking against the gates of hell.[3] We see this in the life of Jesus. There were times when he stood his ground, and there were times he took it. He blitzed the money tables in the temple.[4] He stood when he was led into the wilderness to be tempted by the devil.[5] Jesus struck when he confronted the hypocrisy of the Pharisees.[6] He stood his ground in Gethsemane. Jesus attacked the fig-tree[7] and the demonic, cliff-jumping swine.[8] He stood before Pilate and those who crucified him.

We walk, then stand. We face criticism and all the assaults against us; we don't strike back; we stand, unmoveable and faithful to God and God's word, without retreat or compromise. We turn the other cheek; we do not curse, but we allow God's love to rule in our hearts, even toward those who want to crucify us: 'Father, forgive them.'

I don't look to myself to stand, but I have faith in Christ to stand in and through me. Paul the apostle knew it was impossible without divine help. He tells us what we need to put on if we are going to stand and not fall back into the world or crumble in cowardly retreat. Paul never expected us to stand naked and unarmed. He tells us to reach into our closet and get dressed for battle.

> Finally, be strong in the Lord and in his mighty power. Put on the full armour of God, so that you can take your *stand* against the devil's schemes . . . put on the full armour of God, so that when the day of evil comes, you may be able to *stand your ground*, and

after you have done everything, to *stand*. *Stand firm* then, with the belt of truth buckled round your waist, with the breastplate of righteousness in place, and with your feet fitted with the readiness that comes from the gospel of peace. In addition to all this, take up the shield of faith, with which you can extinguish all the flaming arrows of the evil one. Take the helmet of salvation and the sword of the Spirit, which is the word of God.

And pray in the Spirit on all occasions with all kinds of prayers and requests.

(Eph. 6:10–18, italics mine)

This is how we prepare ourselves to stand, not just attack. We stand in God's truth. We stand firmly assured of our salvation. We stand with a clear conscience. We stand ready to speak the word of God into every situation. We stand in God's peace, not in anger or in frustrated indignation. We stand knowing who we are in Christ. We stand with a shield guarding our hearts and minds against all the lies thrown at us. Above all, it's the words of God that matter, not our arguments, politics or opinions. Think about the way Jesus stood his ground in the wilderness.

Satan wants us to retreat, throw down our armour and run. Jesus tells his disciples how this demonic scheme is often implemented. He knows because he faced it head-on in the wilderness temptation. Jesus told his disciples that it's all about the message, the ways and the words of God. The first thing Satan does is try to rip the word of God out of our hearts. Do you know why Satan is so afraid of the word of God taking root in our lives? It's because it was the word of God that defeated him in the wilderness. When we speak the word in faith, the devils tremble, they even shut up and leave us alone.

> Some people are like seed along the path, where the word is sown. As soon as they hear it, Satan comes and *takes away the word* that was sown in them.
>
> *(Mark 4:15, italics mine)*

Have you ever said, 'Boy, that was a good sermon.' Then, the next day, someone asks you what it was about. At times I hate that question because I have to answer, 'Hmm, I don't remember, but it was inspiring.' Have my brain cells gone rogue, or could this possibly be what Jesus warned his disciples about? I know the word on Sunday inspired me, but I sure can't remember the content. This forgetfulness is probably a sign that there is still some hardness in my heart. Lord, give us ears to hear and to actively guard, protect and possess what we have heard.

If Satan can't steal the word from our minds and hearts, he moves on to stage two. He sends persecution to see if we will continue our stance. What he's hoping for is that we will throw out the word ourselves and not affirm it because of cowardice, failure or self-preservation.

> Others, like seed sown on rocky places, hear the word and at once receive it with joy. But since they have no root, they last only a short time. When trouble or persecution comes *because of the word*, they quickly fall away.
>
> *(Mark 4:16–17, italics mine)*

First, Satan wants to steal the word from us. If he can't yank it out of our hearts and minds, he sends persecution or opposition, hoping we will toss the word out ourselves. For example, 'Oh, I prayed for my sick friend, and they weren't healed. I don't believe God heals today, so I'm not going to pray about it anymore. It doesn't work.' This is how Satan wins the battle for our minds.

So what's Satan going to do if he can't steal the word out of our hearts or get us to throw it out ourselves? What's his strategy if we stand our ground? He switches tactics. Stage three is the most subtle, insidious, and treacherous scheme of the three-step invasion.

> Still others, like seed sown among thorns, hear the word; but the worries of this life, the deceitfulness of wealth and the desires for other things come in and choke the word, making it unfruitful.
>
> *(Mark 4:18–19)*

This scheme has successfully lured and entrapped the human race since our expulsion from Eden. God warned the Hebrew people, 'When you eat and are satisfied, be careful that you do not forget the LORD.'[9] After we have done all to stand, stand!

Life is becoming more complex as the world, government, bureaucracy, provision for our families, and entertainment fill our hearts and minds. These all vie for our attention. If Satan can't steal the word from our hearts, if he can't get us to deny and ignore God's word in the face of persecution, then he leads us down the path, shouting, 'Buy this, buy that; you need that; put your family first; further your career; struggle to the top; answer your phone.' If he can't get the word out of us, he leads us into the brambles and throws more and more fertilizer on the weeds to choke the word of God we hold onto. We still have the word, but it is now handcuffed and chained within a dark cell made from the cares of this world and all its charms.

It's hard to put God and his kingdom first when this world is the major attraction and pull in our lives. As Jesus said, 'Where your treasure is, there your heart will be also.'[10] Suffice it to say, this does not promote an awesome life or draw us into the adventure.

When we say 'yes' to something, we are saying 'no' to other options. Each 'yes' spoken to the world is a 'no' to the kingdom of God.

- I don't have time to pray.
- I have too many other things to do and worry about.
- I can't go to church this morning because the big game is on the tube.

As I said in Chapter 7, if we want more of God, we have to make more room for him in our lives. We cry out. 'More, Lord, more of you.'

God gently whispers, 'More child, give me more to work with.'

Paul told us how to equip ourselves to stand, but why illustrate it with armour? Can you imagine your grandmother standing there, girded up with a shield and sword? I would guess many of us have powerful grandmothers and have been influenced by their love and prayers, but the point Paul is making is that to stand, we have to be militant, determined, focused and aware of our position and our mission in Christ and for his kingdom. The cure for idolatry is not to go off-grid but to 'love the Lord your God with all your heart and with all your soul and with all your mind and with all your strength'.[11] Put off the world and put on the kingdom.

Declare

Being quarantined and isolated during the coronavirus lock-down[1] was not healthy or conducive to spiritual equilibrium, unless you're living in a monastery or have taken a vow of silence. It's easy to drift when so many churches close their doors and go online. Watching a face on a screen is not the same as personal interaction in the same room.

So one day early on, I decided to write myself a decree – something to keep me spiritually focused. It was a statement of faith and purpose in Christ. I often read it to myself. It encapsulates everything written in this book. We may not relate to all of it, but we are growing more into it. Remember, we aren't called to be ordinary people; we are called to be extraordinary.[2] Mediocrity is never celebrated in heaven or on earth. I invite you to read the decree out loud. The Holy Spirit might surprise you.

A Morning Decree

I am a child of the living God. I am his, and he is mine. I am accepted into the family by the blood of Jesus Christ. I am sealed by the Holy Spirit. I am not my own.

I am an ambassador of the kingdom of God. I live before an audience of one. I represent and honour the name of Jesus the Christ above all other names, governments, and institutions.

I am led by the Holy Spirit and the living word of God. The fears and false testimonies of this world do not control or define me.

I am not called to survive, but to stand and conquer. In the power of the Holy Spirit and the resurrected Christ, I do not cower. By faith, I intercede and kick down the gates of hell before me in the name of Jesus Christ. No weapon formed against me prospers. No evil will come near my home this day.

The favour of God is upon me. I steward this favour in honour of his name and for his glory. I celebrate the doors he opens and thank him for closing the ones he chooses to lock. God is my father, and he watches my back. His angels surround me.

My prayers matter. The Holy Spirit teaches and informs me. He shows me the heart of God. My Father listens and answers. We walk this path together.

I stand and embrace God's strength through faith. I refuse to yield to the temptations and lies that try to control and mould me. In the name of Jesus and his word, I will not be a slave to sin or grieve the Holy Spirit. It was for freedom that Christ set me free.

The love of God is my banner. The compassion of Jesus is my motivation. I will share God's love with everyone I meet this day.

My call is not just to proclaim the gospel but to be the gospel – not just to give a message but to be the message. I will encourage and offer hope wherever possible, because love never fails.

By the grace of the Father, in the power of the Holy Spirit, and in the name of Jesus Christ, I will fulfil all God has called me to do this day.

I will abide and dwell in the will of God – nothing less, nothing more, and nothing else. His joy is my strength. His word is my guide. His love is my anchor. My life today will make a difference in this world. Christ lives in me, and I live in him. I am clothed in Christ.

So I say to this day: 'Bring it on!'

Tonight, I will shout, 'Victory!'

Then I will tell the stories of his goodness.

Epilogue

Writing this book has been a joy. It is the story of God's grace and kindness. The experiences, the lessons and the presence of God that have led to this point I find awesome and extremely humbling. These past few years, I have found myself praying these simple words: 'Lord, keep the fountain pure; may the wells we drink from stay true to you.'

There is a lot of deception and compromise in this world, and its reach is not far from any of us or the media we let into our homes. Deception knocks on the doors of the church, our schools, our governments, and even our own minds and hearts. Keeping our spiritual compass set to the truth as we navigate the kingdom we can't see with our natural eyes is a challenge.

Today, truth is a rare commodity, but it was no less an issue at the time of Jesus. Pilate brazenly asked, 'What is truth?'[1] His heart was so hard that he didn't recognize the truth standing right there in front of him, looking him in the eye. Much of the world we navigate today stands in the same camp as Pilate and the Jewish leaders pontificating at that terrible trial.

I often tell myself and others that the best way to avoid deception is not to pray for clarity or divine protection but to be a lover of the truth – even when it hurts and tests us. Jesus gave his disciples this otherworldly lesson.

> I am the way and the truth and the life. No one comes to the Father except through me. If you really know me, you will know my Father as well.

> *(John 14:6–7)*

To Jesus, truth isn't just a doctrine; it's a person. The way is not a law or a treasure map we call the Bible; it is a person. Life – eternal life – is not a detached gift we cling to in hope; it is a person. Anytime we veer away from the person and focus on the product, the waters start to cloud.

If truth is a person, then people need to encounter that individual – not just our defence and explanations about him. People want to know the reality of God. Their eternity-microchip-tracker is beeping more than ever as the world continues to spiral into chaos and mayhem. They may not express it in front of us, but inside they are all looking up and shouting, 'There must be more than this!'

Paul informs us, 'The creation waits in eager expectation for the children of God to be revealed.'[2] Just as Jesus revealed the Father when people encountered him, we are called to do the same. We are to be Christ in this world. As ambassadors of God's kingdom, we are summoned to show them 'the more' they are hoping for is out there beyond space and time.

The world doesn't need additional speeches, ideas or spiritual stories without an encounter with the Holy Spirit to back them – they need an authentic connection with the truth, the risen, living Saviour, Jesus Christ the Word. Yes, we preach the gospel, but the gospel is more than just statements of dogma. It tangibly reveals there is a good King who now sits at the right hand of God the Father, whose name is above all names in heaven and on earth, and he does things. He does miraculous things even today. To those who put their faith in him and his sacrifice on the cross, he declares, 'Not guilty!' We need to put on Christ and walk out of our front doors clothed in the anointing of God's Holy Spirit.

Words without a Holy Spirit revelation and encounter will never free a person from assimilation into this world and the deceptions that entangle. We are not called to hand people a mask but to let Jesus reveal himself in and through us. This is the way Jesus ministered throughout Israel.

> Why then do you accuse me of blasphemy because I said, 'I am God's Son'? *Do not believe me unless I do the works of my Father.* But if I do them, even though you do not believe me, *believe the works*, that you may know and understand that the Father is in me, and I in the Father.
>
> *(John 10:36–8, italics mine)*

This is how Jesus introduced his Father to Israel. We are to be like him. Every one of us, as believers and followers of an otherworldly King, is reborn for this. There are no exceptions. We not only have the green light to live an adventure-driven life, we also have all the resources to jump into the middle of the stream and see where the river takes us. The world needs an encounter with God's awesome people, clothed with Christ and full of the Holy Spirit in them and upon them.

We often hear people talk about the call and the mission of God. I have discovered in my life that it isn't just a call to mission, but a call to adventure. It is an awesome honour and a privilege to step out of the boat and follow when we hear Jesus say, 'Come.' This is what he says to all his children who have the eyes to see and the ears to hear and are not afraid to say, 'Here am I. Send me.'[3]

> Father, in the name of Jesus Christ and in the power and influence of the Holy Spirit, draw us so close to you that our expectation level explodes, as it did with the disciples who walked with you in those early days back in Israel. May the potential you have endowed us with bring heaven to earth. Flood us and our communities with wonder upon wonder. Open our eyes, Lord; we want to see Jesus!

RICHARD CAN BE CONTACTED AT
https://richard-porter.com

Notes

Part One: The Call

1 Chicken in the Car

[1] John 8:23.
[2] John 17:16.
[3] John 18:36.
[4] Matt. 18:3; 19:23–4; Mark 10:24–5; Acts 14:22.
[5] E.g., consider all the denominations and lifestyles we Christians adopt, support, and even argue for and against.
[6] E.g., John 15:11; 17:13; 1 Pet. 1:8.
[7] Phil. 4:7.
[8] The miracles range throughout the Bible: axe heads float, seas part, people are miraculously healed, and then there are the signs and wonders.

2 Shocker

[1] Jack S. Margolis and Richard Clorfene, *A Child's Garden of Grass: The Official Handbook for Marijuana Users* (North Hollywood, CA: Contact Books, 1969).
[2] Puff on marijuana as a cigarette or in a pipe.

3   'A good man brings good things out of the good stored up in his heart, and an evil man brings evil things out of the evil stored up in his heart. For the mouth speaks what the heart is full of' (Luke 6:45).

4   See also Eph. 5:8–10; Gal. 3:27.

5   See also Lev. 11:44; Lev. 19:2.

6   See also Ps. 16:11; Prov. 3:5–6; Isa. 40:31; Jer. 29:11; John 10:10; Rom. 8:28,37; 2 Cor. 12:9; Phil. 4:13.

3 Intolerable Seizure

1   The Horsehead Nebula is a giant cloud of gas and dust located in the Orion constellation. The images from space are stunning. https://en.wikipedia.org/wiki/Horsehead_Nebula (accessed 14 June 2023).

2   'Great fear [awe] seized the whole church and all who heard about these events' (Acts 5:11).

'They were terrified [awed] and asked each other, 'Who is this? Even the wind and the waves obey him!' (Mark 4:41).

'When Jesus had finished saying these things, the crowds were amazed [awed] at his teaching' (Matt. 7:28).

'The crowd was amazed [awed] and said, "Nothing like this has ever been seen in Israel"' (Matt. 9:33).

'Coming to his home town, he began teaching the people in their synagogue, and they were amazed [awed]. "Where did this man get this wisdom and these miraculous powers?" they asked' (Matt. 13:54). See also Matt. 21:20; 22:20–22; and Mark 5:19–20.

3   Some may ask, 'But Jesus said he would never leave me or forsake me, and the Holy Spirit lives inside of me; isn't he always present?' Yes, he is, but God also takes it to another level. In John 20:19–22, Jesus breathes on the disciples and tells them to receive the Holy Spirit. In Acts 1:6–8, Jesus tells them they will receive *power* when the Holy Spirit comes *upon them*.

Then we witness both manifestations in Acts 2:3–4. The glory of God was visibly and tangibly upon them; it shimmered like flames of fire. It seems there are two levels of experience and outworking: the Holy Spirit in us and the Holy Spirit upon us. The Holy Spirit at times came upon the saints of the Old Testament for power. They did extraordinary things because of the Spirit upon them but, as yet, the Holy Spirit wasn't in them. The Holy Spirit dwells in every Christian for ever, but the Spirit isn't always upon us. We can quench the Holy Spirit and live in the flesh. The anointing of the Spirit comes when the Spirit is both in us and upon us. This is what I mean by the tangible presence of God. We welcome Jesus into every day and moment of our lives, and we know he is with us, not as a biblical doctrine but as a tangible, experiential reality. The tangible presence has to do with a knowing, a deep spiritual awareness and connection, and a profound sense of God's companionship, love, and faithfulness. At times, his presence is overwhelming; other times, his presence is a quiet peace and assurance. Perhaps you can explain this better than I can, but hopefully it will become clear as you read through the pages of this book. I am pleased you made it this far.

4 Oil Shortage

[1]   TED stands for technology, entertainment and design.
[2]   Matt. 22:11.
[3]   Luke 15:11–32.
[4]   Matt. 25:1–13.
[5]   Matt. 25:8.
[6]   Matt. 25:9.
[7]   E.g. John 15:1–8; 1 Thess. 5:16–24; Col. 2:6; 3:1–3; 1 John 2:24,27; 3:24; 4:13.
[8]   For further reading, I would suggest the classic by Brother Lawrence, *The Practice of the Presence of God* (New Kensington: Whitaker, 1982). For a more contemporary book, consider Bill

Johnson, *Hosting the Presence: Unveiling Heaven's Agenda* (Shippensburg: Destiny Image, 2012).

9   Exod. 33:1–3.
10 Exod. 33:17.
11 E.g., Ps. 103:7; Exod. 20:18–19.

5 Wonder upon Wonder

1   This is what they will get in return for their pride,
        for insulting and mocking
        the people of the LORD Almighty.
    The LORD will be awesome to them
        when he destroys all the gods of the earth.
    Distant nations will bow down to him,
        all of them in their own lands.

                                                (Zeph. 2:10–11)

2   John 10:28.

6 Ticket to Ride

1   David Wilkerson (1931–2011), was an evangelical, prophetic pastor and the founder of Teen Challenge (a worldwide addiction rehab programme). He is also the author of *The Cross and the Switchblade* (New York: Pyramid, 1962), *The Vision* (New York: Jove, 1974), and other books.

2   Jackie Pullinger (1944–), is a missionary working among the Triads (an organized crime syndicate) in the walled city of Hong Kong. The incredible story of her early work is recorded in her book, *Chasing the Dragon* (London: Hodder & Stoughton, 1980).

3   John Wesley (1703–91) was an evangelist, author, theologian, cleric and the founder of the Methodist Church.

4   George Mueller (1805–98) was an evangelist, pastor, and director of the Asley Down Orphanage in Bristol, England. He was one of the founders of the Plymouth Brethren movement.

5   Rees Howells (1879–1950) was a Welsh missionary, intercessor, and founder of the Bible College of Wales.

6   Smith Wigglesworth (1859–1947) was an evangelist and saw many people miraculously healed during his ministry.

7   During the Jesus movement – the last great American revival – when thousands of hippies turned to Jesus, many in the church didn't know what to do with them. I have heard stories that make me weep about pastors turning real converts away because they didn't fit in or meet the pastor's expectations.

8   Norman Grubb, *Rees Howells: Intercessor* (London: Lutterworth Press, 1954), pp. 173–4.

9   Jas 2:17.

7 Green Light

1   The resurrection was the beginning. Christians vigorously celebrate the cross and resurrection event but we kind of run out of steam when it comes to the ascension. However, the ascension is the culmination of the cross event – the second half of Jesus' journey home. Jesus is the name above all names because he is now seated at the right hand of the Father. He is the head of the divine council. From his exalted position, he can send the Holy Spirit to dwell in us. The cross brought us forgiveness and restoration, but the ascension took salvation to a whole new level – the life of God in every believer. This is why the Bible says we are seated with him in heavenly places; Jesus, ascended into heaven as fully God and fully human. The ascension seals what Jesus did on the cross and the resurrection. Thank God that Jesus didn't just rise from the dead; he also ascended into heaven in his human body, to rule and intercede on our behalf. I thank God for the ascension of Christ.

2   Lev. 6:13.
3   Rev. 3:14–16.
4   Matt. 8:10; 15:21–8; Mark 12:41–4.

Part Two: The Wardrobe

10 Masks in the Closet

1   Gal. 5:22–3.
2   Ned Flanders is a cartoon character in a TV series called *The Simpsons.*
3   Heb. 4:1–13.

11 Put It On

1   But what about verses like 2 Peter 1:5: 'For this very reason, *make every effort to add to your faith*' (italics mine)? The point is that faith comes first. It's the foundation we build on. There are many other verses in the Bible telling us to actively strive with determination. For example: Luke 13:24; 2 Pet. 1:10; 3:14; Rom. 14:19; Eph. 4:1–3; Heb. 4:9–11; 12:1,14; but it's never from the position of self-effort as opposed to faith in Christ. By faith, we purposefully act on God's promises. Through faith in him working through us, we step out and live the life and do the deeds. Those who haven't yet turned to Christ may strive to do good and exhibit many of the attributes listed in the Bible, but that doesn't mean they have put on Christ. They are similar to the five virgins, who started well but ran out of oil in the long haul. Self-effort only takes us so far, but not far enough (Matt. 25:1–13). 'For all have sinned and *fall short* of the glory of God' (Rom. 3:23, italics mine). Our lives stem from Christ, who lives

in us. The Christian life is not just a mental and physical exercise we put into action because we happened to read about it in the Bible. Consider the Old Testament law. The ancient Jews had the law but not the indwelling Holy Spirit. Their history shows how difficult this was for them. We can't live the life of Christ without his continual presence. We have this treasure, 'Christ in us', but we must also put him on by faith. Biblically, the New Testament talks about it as a struggle between flesh and spirit. The flesh operates outside of Christ; the Spirit is triggered by our faith in Christ. For example, look at Gal. 5:16–25; Rom. 6:12–13; 7:18; 8:6–9; 13:14; Matt. 26:41; Heb. 13:21; and Phil. 4:13.

2   Rom. 12:2; 2 Cor 10:5.

3   Jesus told Nicodemus that no one can see the kingdom of God unless they are born again (John 3:3). The Pharisee was blind to the spiritual opportunities around him. Religion and strenuous self-effort caged him.

4   Eph. 6:10–11.

5   Eph. 4:24; Col. 3:10.

6   1 Cor. 12:4–11.

7   1 Cor. 6:19; Titus 2:14.

8   John 15:1–5. Also, consider what Jesus said in his great prayer prior to the cross: 'Now this is eternal life: that they know you, the only true God, and Jesus Christ, whom you have sent' (John 17:3).

9   John 14:6.

10   John 1:1.

11   Heb. 2:1–4.

12   Phil. 4:13.

13   Eph. 2:8–10.

12 Follow the Smoke

1   E.g., 1 John 4:7–13.

13 Take It Off

[1] This is comparable to the Borg in *Star Trek*. They were the scariest nasties in the universe because no one could defeat them. Their goal was to assimilate all their victims and rip away their true identities.

14 Anointed Threads

[1] 'Persecution Blog' *The Voice of the Martyrs* (2015) https://www.persecutionblog.com/2015/05/people-of-the-cross.html (accessed 12 Dec. 2022).

[2] E.g., Lev. 21:10; 10:1–7; Ps. 133:2–3; and Luke 24:49. In these few examples, and many others throughout the Scriptures, the garments are an extension of the person. The anointing of the Holy Spirit works through the attachments of the anointed person; whether it be clothing, the staff in the hand of Moses, or even our shadow. 'People brought those who were ill into the streets and laid them on beds and mats so that at least Peter's shadow might fall on some of them as he passed by. Crowds gathered also from the towns around Jerusalem, bringing those who were ill and those tormented by impure spirits, and all of them were healed' (Acts 5:15–16).

[3] 2 Kgs 2:9.

[4] 1 Kgs 19:19; 2 Kgs 2:9.

[5] 2 Kgs 2:8–14.

[6] The hem of a garment was the most ornate part of the vestment. The greater the prestige, the more elaborate the embroidery.

[7] Mari is a significant archaeology site in present-day Syria that hosted a vast library uncovering the customs and practises of the region. It's a valuable resource for Old Testament studies.

[8] Victor H. Matthews, 'The Anthropology of Clothing in the Joseph Narrative', *Journal for the Study of the Old Testament* 65 (1995): pp. 25–36.

⁹ Jacob Milgrom, 'Of Hems and Tassels', *Biblical Archaeology Review*, Vol. IX, No. 3 (1983): pp. 61–5.

¹⁰ 1 Sam. 24:1–7.

¹¹ Joseph receives a garment from his father. His brothers take it off of him and sell Joseph into slavery. At the end of the story, Pharoah clothes Joseph. Then Joseph ironically clothes the brothers who betrayed him (Gen. 45:22). Follow the story through Genesis 37 – 50.

¹² Ora Horn Prouser, 'Suited to the Throne: The Symbolic Use of Clothing in the David and Saul Narratives', *Journal for the Study of the Old Testament* 71 (1996): pp. 27–37.

¹³ E.g., 1 Sam. 15:27–8; 17:38–9; 18:3–4; 21:9; 31:9.

¹⁴ See also Isa. 20:1–6. Isaiah walked the streets naked for about three years as a prophetic illustration.

¹⁵ E.g., Gen. 37:29,34; 44:12–13; Lev. 10:1–7; 13:45; 21:10; Num. 14:1–9; Isa. 36:22; Joel 2:13; Matt. 26:65. To tear your clothes was a symbolic act of exposure. In the face of death, sin, frustration, and anger, you strip off what your garment represents and face life at the core of your being, your basic humanity without the trappings.

15 Twilight Zone

¹ An American television franchise created by Rod Serling.

² 2 Cor. 5:3–4.

³ E.g., Gen. 3:7–11; 9:23; 2 Sam. 6:20; Lam. 1:8; Ezek. 16:7–8,36–7; Hos. 2:3; Mic. 1:11; Mark 14:52; Rev. 3:17; 16:15; 17:16.

⁴ Num. 20:26.

⁵ 1 Sam. 31:8–10.

⁶ Ezek. 16:39.

⁷ Isa. 45:1.

⁸ Job 12:17–19; 19:9–10; Jer. 13:22.

⁹ Job 1:21.

10 E.g., Rev. 16:15.
11 Gen. 3:21.
12 Luke 15:20–22.
13 Eph. 4:22–4.
14 See also Matt. 22:1–14; Isa. 61:10; Rev. 3:4; 19:7–8.
15 Eph. 6:10–17.
16 Eph. 4:25.
17 Eph. 4:28.
18 Eph. 4:31–32.

16 Art of Growing Up

1 I have read about this somewhere, but I am unable to locate the source. I am not an historian, and I apologize if I have been misguided. I have searched the internet but haven't found any references describing this practice. However, it doesn't at all discredit the point this illustration is making with regard to our entitlement and the process of living up to our responsibility.
2 E.g., 1 Cor. 1:30.
3 Matt. 6:19–21.
4 Luke 2:52.
5 E.g., 1 John 1:9.
6 Heb. 12:1–3.
7 Phil. 1:6.
8 John 15:1–17.
9 John 16:8.
10 Rom. 8:13.
11 1 John 1:9.
12 See also Heb. 12:1–3.

Part Three: The Matrix

18 What's It All About?

[1] Scholars argue that the author of Ecclesiastes is some unnamed person called 'the teacher'. This may be true, but it is irrelevant. Whether the author is King Solomon or some other Jewish sage posing as Solomon (which cannot be categorically proved one way or the other), we need to keep in mind that the book of Ecclesiastes is intended to be read, interpreted and understood from Solomon's perspective.

[2] 1 Kgs 10:14–29.

[3] 1 Kgs 10:27.

[4] 1 Kgs 10:1–9,24.

[5] Eccl. 1:1–18.

[6] Eccl. 2:7. Solomon calls them slaves, but slavery in Israel was not like the slavery of other nations or modern practice. It was comparable to indentured servitude – not domination.

[7] Solomon calls them the 'treasure of kings and provinces' (Eccl. 2:8).

[8] 1 Kgs 4:26; Eccl. 2:7.

[9] Eccl. 2:4–9.

[10] 1 Kgs 11:1–8; Eccl. 2:8.

[11] Eccl. 12:13–14.

19 Divine Microchip

[1] Pete Seeger wrote this song in the late 1950s.

[2] This discussion is expanded in Chapter 34.

[3] E.g., Matt. 5:6; John 4:13–14; 6:35.

20 Face in the Mirror

1 'You are my friends if you do what I command' (John 15:14).
2 E.g., Gen. 9:6.
3 Gen. 3:7.
4 There are basically three schools of thought regarding the image of God. The substantive view focuses on the various characteristics unique to humanity, such as rationality, morality and spiritual awareness. The relational view focuses on our relationship to God: how close we are to him in our lives and commitment. The functional view concentrates on our role in caring for Eden, the wildlife and the planet.
5 E.g., Eph. 4:24; Col. 3:10.
6 E.g., Gen. 1:26; Ps. 8.
7 E.g., Gerhard von Rad, *Genesis: A Commentary* (trans. John H. Marks; The Old Testament Library; Philadelphia: Westminster Press, 1961), p. 56; John Piper, 'The Image of God', *Desiring God* (1971), https://www.desiringgod.org/articles/the-image-of-god#fn8 (accessed 16 Dec. 2023); Alon Goshen Gottstein, 'The Body as Image of God in Rabbinic Literature', *Harvard Theological Review* 87 (1994): pp. 171–95.
8 E.g., Deut. 4:13; Luke 24:39; John 4:24; Col. 1:15; 1 Tim. 1:17.
9 E.g., Gen. 5:3; Ezek. 1:26. See also D.J.A. Clines, 'The Image of God in Man', *Tyndale Bulletin* 19 (1968): pp. 53–103; and Richard S. Briggs, 'Humans in the Image of God and Other Things Genesis Does Not Make Clear', *Journal of Theological Interpretation*, 4.1 (2010): pp. 111–126. These two articles trace the history of interpretation regarding the image of God in humanity. The major commentaries on Genesis also address the subject.
10 When God is portrayed with body parts and a human disposition, we call it an andromorphic projection; a vision we can relate to but that doesn't communicate the reality. However, let's not be too quick to land the plane on this runway.
11 The Hebrew word *tselem* (image) is frequently used in the Bible to point out a physical likeness, e.g. Gen. 5:3. Consider also, Exod. 33:20; Col. 1:15.
12 John 4:24; Luke 24:39.

13 Acts 1:9–11.
14 In the gospels, he said it around eighty times, e.g., Matt. 12:8; Mark 8:31; Luke 7:34; and John 6:27.
15 Heb. 1:3.
16 Col. 1:15; John 14:9–11.
17 2 Cor. 4:4.
18 Rom. 8:29.
19 Just a small observation: No matter how we interpret the image of God in Genesis, the New Testament takes it to another level in the light of Jesus Christ, the second Adam.
20 See Benjamin D. Sommer, *The Bodies of God and the World of Ancient Israel* (Cambridge: Cambridge University Press, 2009).
21 'When he opened the fifth seal, I saw under the altar the souls of those who had been slain because of the word of God and the testimony they had maintained' (Rev. 6:9). This Scripture is talking about an interim position. I am not saying these martyred souls are not human, but they are not fully clothed as humans. They will receive new bodies, but for the time being, God clothes them with 'white robes' (Rev. 6:11).
22 See also 1 Cor. 15:42–4; Rom. 8:18–23.

21 Slow the Descent

1 Matt. 17:1–3.
2 E.g., Luke 5:1–11; Matt. 8:23–7; Mark 6:45–52; 11:12–14; John 21:4–11.
3 E.g., Matt. 8:18; Luke 9:10–17; John 2:1–11.
4 E.g., Luke 4:28–30; Mark 12:17; Luke 22:49–51; John 18:4–9.
5 E.g., Matt. 14:14; 15:32; 18:27; 20:34; Mark 1:41; 5:19; 6:34; Luke 7:13.
6 E.g., John 5:19; 7:16–18; 12:49; 14:10.
7 Gen. 1:31 – 2:2.
8 Matt. 25:41; Luke 10:18.
9 E.g., Luke 10:18; Job 1 – 2; Rev. 12:9–12.
10 E.g., Rev. 20:1–3; 2 Pet. 2:4.

[11] 2 Pet. 2:4.

[12] Rev. 20:10–15.

[13] Eph. 6:12.

[14] E.g., Col. 3:1; Heb. 11:9–16,24–6.

[15] E.g., 1 John 2:15–17.

[16] Phil. 4:8–9.

[17] Isa. 5:20.

[18] E.g., 2 Thess. 2:5–7.

[19] Rom. 3:23.

[20] For further discussion, see Dane C. Ortlund, 'What Does it Mean to Fall Short of the Glory of God? Romans 3:23 in Biblical-Theological Perspective', *Westminster Theological Journal* 80 (2018): pp. 121–40.

[21] See Haley G. Jacob, *Conformed to the Image of His Son: Reconsidering Paul's Theology of Glory in Romans* (Downers Grove: InterVarsity Press, 2018).

[22] The word 'sin' is often used as a noun and not a verb. Eg., Gen. 4:7; Rom. 3:23; 1 John 3:4; Jas 1:15.

[23] To Paul, the mind of Christ is the message of the cross. See Gordon D. Fee, *The First Epistle to the Corinthians* (Grand Rapids, MI: Eerdmans, 1987): pp. 117–120.

[24] 1 John 4:19.

22 Reality Gauge

[1] SETI (Search for Extraterrestrial Intelligence) is a large collective of scientists and interested individuals monitoring the airwaves and electromagnetic radiation, hoping to make contact with citizens of distant planets. Check out the movie *Contact*.

[2] Eph. 2:10.

[3] Isa. 64:8.

23 Be Christ in the Room

[1] John 4:1–42.
[2] E.g., John 5:19–20.
[3] E.g., Luke 1:35; 3:22; 4:14; 24:49; Acts 1:8.
[4] 2 Cor. 4:7.
[5] Rev. 1:8; 22:13.
[6] 1 Cor. 6:19.
[7] Col. 1:27.

Part Four: The Identity

24 Sword of Freedom

[1] The National Wallace Monument in Stirling, Scotland.
[2] 'God demonstrates his own love for us in this: while we were still sinners, Christ died for us' (Rom. 5:8).
[3] John 6:3,13,32–5.
[4] John 8:23.
[5] 'All of us who were baptised into Christ Jesus were baptised into his death? We were therefore buried with him through baptism into death' (Rom. 6:3–4).

   'For we know that our old self was crucified with him so that the body ruled by sin might be done away with' (Rom. 6:6).

   'For you died, and your life is now hidden with Christ in God' (Col. 3:3).

   'I have been crucified with Christ and I no longer live' (Gal. 2:20).
[6] Rom. 12:1–2.
[7] E.g., John 10:27; 16:13–15; Heb. 3:7.
[8] 'They are not of the world, even as I am not of it' (John 17:14–16).

25 Who are You?

1 Acts 24:5.
2 Acts 11:25–6.
3 E.g., Friedrich Nietzsche: 'Show me that you are redeemed, and I will believe in your redeemer.'
4 1 Cor. 3:18–23.
5 1 Cor. 13:8.
6 Rom. 14:4.
7 John 3:3; 14:17.
8 E.g., Acts 8:18–25.
9 E.g., John 3:16–18; 1 Cor. 15:1–11.
10 Matt. 5:13.
11 Matt. 5:14; Eph. 5:7–14.
12 1 Cor. 9:24–7.
13 Heb. 11:13–16; 1 Pet. 2:11.
14 E.g., 2 Sam. 10:1–5; 1 Chr. 19:1–5; 2 Chr. 36:16; Matt. 14:1–12; 21:35–9; 23:34–7; Rev. 11:7.

26 I Pledge Allegiance

1 John 18:36.
2 Phil. 3:4–6; Acts 22:28–9.
3 Acts 9:1–19. See Rom. 11:8; Gal. 2:8.
4 Eccl. 1:2.
5 Gal. 1:11–24.
6 Acts: 13:44–8.
7 2 Cor. 5:20.
8 If you are interested, you can read about it in chapter 1 of my previous book: *The Kingdom of God, the Director's Cut: Understanding the Greatest Show on Earth* (Bletchley, Milton Keynes: Authentic, 2021).
9 Phil. 3:3–14.

27 Kingdom Accountability

[1] E.g., see Herodotus, *Histories* [book VII, ch. 133–4]; Harold G. Nicolson, *The Evolution of Diplomatic Method* (Leicester: University of Leicester Press, 1998); Linda S. Frey and Marsha L. Frey, *The History of Diplomatic Immunity* (Columbus: Ohio State University Press, 1999); 'Diplomatic Immunity', *Wikipedia* https://en.wikipedia.org/wiki/Diplomatic_immunity#cite_ref-6 (accessed 5 Jan. 2023).

[2] Eph. 6:12.

[3] Mark 14:29–31.

[4] 1 Cor. 1:24.

[5] E.g., Matt. 19:16–22; John 6:60–66.

[6] 1 Cor. 3:18–23.

28 True to His Word

[1] Matt. 23:37.

[2] Rev. 21:8.

[3] Acts 7:1–53.

[4] Rom 8:28.

[5] Luke 16:10.

[6] E.g., Ezek. 3:18–19; Prov. 31:9; Eph. 5:11; 1 Pet. 3:15–16; Acts 18:9–10.

[7] I found these two books worth reading: *The New Foxe's Book of Martyrs* and Richard Wurmbrand's *Tortured for Christ.*

[8] Matt. 10:28.

[9] Matt. 16:24.

[10] Rom. 8:17.

29 Heaven's Lesson

[1] This prayer was inspired by the life of George Mueller. If you want to read about an awesome life, read his story.

31 Heaven's Priority

[1] E.g., Gen. 22:1–24; Deut. 8:2,16; Ps. 66:10; Job 23:10; Jer. 17:10; Zech. 13:9; Luke 4:1–13; Jas 1:2,12; 1 Pet. 1:6–7; 4:12–13.

Part Five: The Snapshots

32 Look

[1] See Richard Porter, *The Kingdom of God, The Director's Cut: Understanding the Greatest Show on Earth* (Bletchley, Milton Keynes: Authentic, 2021), pp. 56–7.

[2] Mark 6:49.

[3] Mark 8:5–8.

[4] Mark 8:11–13.

[5] E.g., Exod. 33:12–13; Ps. 103:7.

[6] Mark 8:29.

[7] After Jesus rebuked the disciples for not understanding the message of the two feeding miracles, he and the disciples encountered a blind man. What's of special interest is that Jesus had to pray for this blind person twice before he could see (Mark 8:22–6). This is the only time in the New Testament where Jesus had to pray twice for someone to be healed. The story is a commentary on what was going on with the disciples. They, too, were blind spiritually, and Jesus had to show them the miracle of the loaves twice before their eyes were opened. The paragraph that follows the blind man's healing is Peter's declaration that Jesus is the Messiah.

[8] Gen. 28:16–17.

33 Listen

[1] 'If you are pleased with me, teach me your ways so I may know you and continue to find favour with you' (Exod. 33:13). See also: Pss. 24:3–4; 25:8–12; 67:2; 77:13; 81:13; 95:10 and 103:7, etc.

[2] Consider the words of Jesus: 'My prayer is not for them alone. I pray also for those who will believe in me through their message, that all of them may be one, *Father, just as you are in me and I am in you. May they also be in us* so that the world may believe that you have sent me. I have given them the glory that you gave me, that they may be one as we are one – *I in them and you in me* – so that they may be brought to complete unity. Then the world will know that you sent me and have loved them even as you have loved me' (John 17:20–23, italics mine). See also Eph. 5:31–3.

[3] Read John 17:20–25.

[4] E.g., Matt. 25:1–13; John 3:29; Mark 2:19; Eph. 5:22–33; Rev. 21:2,9–10. In the New Testament, the Church is the bride of Christ; In the Old Testament, the Jewish nation is the wife of YHWH.

[5] 1 Kgs. 19:12.

[6] This is in reference to Chapter 30.

[7] E.g., John 10:14–16.

35 Pray

[1] The church I served at was Sharpe Memorial Church of the Nazarene. I lived at 1444 Gallowgate, Parkhead Cross.

[2] E.g., Eph. 6:18; Jude 1:20.

[3] Luke 23:34.

[4] Acts 7:60.

36 Love

[1] John 21:15–19.

37 Worship

1 Rev. 1:4.
2 https://www.ihopkc.org/.
3 1 Chr. 15:1–18,27; 2 Chr. 8:14–15.
4 E.g., Alexander Akimites and the Sleepless Ones. Bangor monastery, in Northern Ireland, prayed and worshipped 24/7 for about 200 years. David Yonggi Cho set up a 24/7 worship and prayer centre at his international Prayer Mountain retreat in South Korea, and Mike Bickle founded the IHOP (International House of Prayer) in Kansas City.
5 Luke 2:37.
6 Matt. 12:34.
7 John 17:4.
8 Luke 23:46.

38 Obey

1 E.g., Gal. 1:15–20.
2 Mark 1:13.
3 Ezek. 1:1.
4 Isa. 6.
5 'Love language' is a popular psychological expression describing the different ways we perceive or respond to love. The usual five listed are: words of affirmation, acts of service, gifts, quality time and physical touch.
6 John 14:15.
7 Lev. 16:21–2.
8 Luke 4:14–15.
9 Heb. 5:8.
10 Heb. 12:3–4.
11 Luke 2:52.
12 John 15:15.

39 Think

[1] Some congregations have stopped upgrading and are stuck in a cultural time warp. There is nothing wrong with this, but it doesn't promote growth.
[2] Rom. 12:2.
[3] Phil. 4:8.
[4] E.g., Deut. 6:4–9; Isa. 26:3; Col. 3:2.
[5] Prov. 4:23.
[6] John 12:6.
[7] 1 Cor. 15:33.

40 Laugh

[1] Neh. 8:10.
[2] John 15:11.
[3] Heb. 1:9.
[4] Heb. 12:2.
[5] According to the NIV Bible translation.
[6] See Chapter 11.
[7] Rom. 12:15.
[8] Acts 16:16–40.
[9] Consider what this means. They are stripped and immediately lose status. They are going down, although I believe when we are demoted on earth for the sake of Jesus, we are promoted in heaven. I am more concerned about being promoted by God than I am about any earthly promotion. One is temporal, the other is eternal.
[10] Jas 1:2.
[11] 1 Thess. 4:13.

41 Give

[1] In the following verses, the underlying Hebrew phrase is either a 'good eye' or an 'evil eye'. Deut. 28:53–7; Prov. 22:9; 23:6; 28:21–2.
[2] Matt. 6:3.
[3] Matt. 6:19–20.
[4] Mark 12:41–44; Luke 21:1–4.

42 Serve

[1] Read the first chapter of J.R.R. Tolkien's classic, *The Hobbit*.
[2] Mark 10:41.
[3] E.g., Luke 22:24.
[4] E.g., Mark 10:38–40.
[5] I'm not saying that the presidency is not an act of service; I'm just making a contrast between a highly honoured and visible position compared to serving without the kudos or the accolades.
[6] I have read a few different versions of this parable on the internet, but I can't find the source. The way I tell this story is original, but the concept isn't my idea. I put it in this book because it is so applicable to the subject.
[7] Kingdom of God.

43 Restore

[1] E.g., John 5:8–9; Acts 3:6–8.
[2] E.g., Matt. 9:1–8; Mark 1:25–28.
[3] John 9:6–7.
[4] Luke 7:1–10.
[5] Acts 3:5–7.
[6] Acts 5:15–16.
[7] Acts 19:11–12.

44 Walk

1 To grieve the Spirit, in its wider context, has to do with character, godliness, a holy life, and a holy lifestyle – stop sinning. To quench the Spirit is more than just ignoring the gifts and the manifestations of power; it is also opposing and decrying any movement of the Holy Spirit because it doesn't fit comfortably into our expectations or doctrinal position and interpretation. For further reading, consider William DeArteaga, *Quenching the Spirit: Examining Centuries of Opposition to the Moving of the Holy Spirit* (Lake Mary, Florida: Creation House, 1992).

2 1 Cor. 12:1–11.

3 This is an excerpt from 'St Patrick's Breastplate', which is a prayer.

4 2 Tim. 3:5.

45 Stand

1 E.g., Deut. 31:6; Josh. 8:1; Ps. 23:4; Isa. 35:4; 41:10; Jer. 42:11; 46:27; Matt. 10:26,28; Luke 2:10; 1 John 4:18.

2 Acts 2:42–43.

3 Matt. 16:17–20.

4 John 2:15.

5 Luke 4:1–12.

6 Matt. 23.

7 Mark 11:20–25.

8 Matt. 8:28–34.

9 Deut. 6:11–12.

10 Matt. 6:21.

11 Mark 12:30.

46 Declare

[1] 'Timeline of UK government coronavirus lockdowns and restrictions', *Institute for Government* https://www.instituteforgovernment.org.uk/charts/uk-government-coronavirus-lockdowns (accessed 10 Jan. 2023).

[2] E.g., 1 Pet. 2:9.

Epilogue

[1] John 18:38.

[2] Rom. 8:19.

[3] Isa. 6:8.

The Kingdom of God
– The Director's Cut

*Understanding the greatest show
on earth*

Richard Porter

Jesus taught us to pray for God's kingdom to come. But do we understand what we are praying for and what the kingdom of God really looks like?

Using the analogy of God as the director of the greatest show on earth, Richard Porter shows how the kingdom of God is the overarching storyline throughout the Bible. Each scene, from the people of Israel to Jesus and the early church, reveals kingdom truths that impact the church today.

As the story unfolds, you will understand why Jesus proclaimed the message of the kingdom and why it is indeed good news for our towns, our cities, our homes and our families.

978-1-78893-169-4

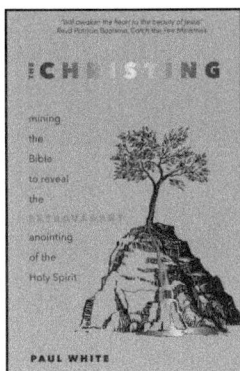

The Christing

*Mining the Bible to reveal
the extravagant anointing
of the Holy Spirit*

Paul White

Do you want to fall more in love with Jesus?

The Holy Spirit is the Spirit of Jesus. The awesome power of
this 'Christing' is to get the life-giving, oppression-busting, free-
dom-bringing life of Jesus into the whole world, starting right where
we live.

Take a gallop through the scriptures with Paul White and discover
the different images used to describe the Holy Spirit. In a fresh and
conversational style, peppered with personal stories and the author's
own illustrations, you will see how the same dynamic power of God
seen throughout the Bible is still available to us today.

Be encouraged to live in a deep, passionate relationship with Jesus.
Get ready to release the 'Christing'!

978-1-78893-173-1

Authentic

We trust you enjoyed reading this book
from Authentic. If you want to be
informed of any new titles from this author
and other releases you can sign up to the
Authentic newsletter by scanning below:

Online:
authenticmedia.co.uk

Follow us: